THROUGH AFRICA...

with Grit, Determination, Guile
and a Modicum of Stupidity

Richard Merrick Jones

LAYOUT AND DESIGN BY:
Papillon Graphics & Design
Toronto, Ontario, Canada M5C 3A6
E-mail: papillongd@home.com
Web Site: members.home.net/papillongd

PDF FORMAT BY:
Virginia West, West End Design
Toronto, Ontario, Canada

PRINTED AND BOUND BY:
InstaBook Canada
30 Community Ave, Unit #2
Stoney Creek, ON
L8E 2Y2
Web Site: www.instabook.ca

Canadian Cataloguing in Publication Data

Jones, Richard Merrick, 1947-
    Through Africa... with grit, determination, guile and a modicum
of stupidity

ISBN 0-9684857-0-7

    1. Africa–Description and travel. 2. Jones, Richard Merrick,
1947–Journeys–Africa. I. Title

DT12.25.J65 1999   916.04'327   C99-900122-1

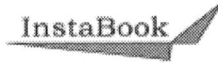

InstaBooks are distributed and printed through:

INSTABOOK

For more information write to:

InstaBook Corporation
1325 NW 9th Ave
Gainesville, Fl. 32605

www.instabook.net

InstaBook Canada, division of DM Industries Inc.

30 Community Ave, Unit #2
Stoney Creek, ON
L8E 2Y2

www.instabook.ca

Insta Book

PRINTED AND BOUND IN CANADA

.

Acknowledgements

The author gratefully acknowledges the following photograph contributors: Philip Corcos, Michael Dowler, Sheila and Robert McComb (Africa) and Alex Clark (Scotland).

He also wishes to highlight the collaboration of Jean Donaldson Jones, who contributed significantly to the preparation of this book.

Special thanks are due to Stéphane Pominville of Papillon Graphics & Design for his creativity, advice and assistance in the production of this work.

Table of Contents

This book is dedicated to
Viv, Robin, Phil and
all the wonderful people
we met on our travels.

.

Introduction

True to the "Trekky" philosophy: to travel, seek out and learn about other countries and cultures were lifelong dreams of both Jean and I, and so, being young and mobile without children or other responsibilities, we set off on what was originally to be an around-the-world tour. Instead, the trip proved to be a fascinating and memorable journey through Africa, covering about 10,000 miles and taking nearly a year to complete.

Many books have been published about Africa. However, one element missing from many of the accounts I have read is the relating of personal experiences in travel, and so this is perhaps the key rationale for the production of this work. It is a documentary of our day-to-day experiences and impressions as we traversed the continent, and I trust it will provide entertainment value for those interested in faraway, exotic places.

The Journey Begins

"One of the last true adventures left in the world." These were the words Robin used to describe the overland trek from Morocco to Kenya. At the outset, my wife, Jean and I had no idea where our travels would take us. We had always said that while we were young we would like to see more of the world, and so in July 1971, only two months after our marriage in Toronto, we sold our belongings and were aboard a plane bound for Britain.

The extent of our planning for this adventure consisted of our savings (about $8,000 Canadian, half of which was to be spent on a vehicle) and the naive idea that we would attempt to travel around the world over the course of the next two years.

On arrival at Gatwick Airport outside of London, England, we immediately boarded a northbound train to Manchester where we planned to purchase a new van directly from the Ford plant. We reasoned that the factory price had to be less than that charged by an automobile dealership. Once in possession of a vehicle, our plan was to travel leisurely through northern England and then on to Scotland where Jean's family lived. But you know what they say about best-laid plans. On our arrival in Manchester we were surprised to learn that due to a backlog of dealership orders, it would take two to three weeks to take delivery of a van. Unwilling to spend both time and money in Manchester, we decided to buy a ticket to Edinburgh and headed north again on the next available train.

Two days later, we arrived in the city of Falkirk, Scotland,

20 miles west of Edinburgh. It was there that I had the thrill of my first double-deck bus ride as we made our way from the city to Jean's parents' home in the tiny village of Rumford. I must admit to being both fascinated and amused by the sight of the bus conductor who dispensed tickets by cranking a lever on the side of a box, strapped to her waist; the scene reminded me of an organ grinder minus the monkey.

A short time later we arrived at the Donaldson residence, but to our dismay, the place was locked and in darkness. It was only then that we realized what had happened. In our haste to leave Manchester, we had forgotten to contact any of Jean's relatives to inform them that our plans had changed, and that we would be arriving a week earlier than originally scheduled. The houses were set so close to each other that a next-door neighbour heard us discussing our predicament and came outside to tell us that Jean's parents had gone on holiday for a few days with the rest of the family, all that is except for one sister, Isa. Perhaps she would have a key for the house. Fortunately for us, Isa, like her other two sisters, lived close by her parents, and so after a 30-minute walk we were at her door. The good news was that Isa was home; the bad news was that she didn't have a key, so we all trouped back to the Donaldson home to see how we could gain entry.

What happened next seemed surreal. As we proceeded to break in at the side entrance of the house, the same kindly neighbour began to make tea and sandwiches for the amateur burglars. First, we tried to pry open the front and rear windows of the house, but they had been locked. (Isa remembered that her father, Robert, had a habit of not only locking windows but screwing them shut when on extended absences.) We then decided to get in by breaking a small bathroom window that was just large enough for the petite

Isa to climb through. A few moments later, just as Isa slipped head first through the toilet window, two of Britain's "finest" arrived on the scene. Apparently, as the neighbour on one side had been feeding us, lending ladders and offering advice, the neighbour on the other side had been calling the police.

Politely but firmly, they asked us why we were loitering about the Donaldson residence. Jean and I had just begun to stammer our way through some sort of an explanation when Isabel popped her head out of the bathroom window and casually said, "oh, hello John, hello Alex," to the policemen, as though it was an everyday occurrence to be caught breaking into a house at midnight. Eventually, after we had explained the situation, Alex and John helped us to remove the locks from the front door. We were fortunate that Isabel had known the pair, but then that shouldn't have been too much of a surprise since everyone knew just about everyone else in this small community. Declining an offer of tea, or even a drink of duty-free Scotch, the two smiling policemen departed, and Jean and I were left marvelling at how accommodating the Scottish police force had been.

During the week that followed, while we awaited the return of Jean's parents, we repaired the front door locks and the broken window, exchanged Canadian dollars for British pounds sterling and purchased a new, four-cylinder, Austin-Morris van from a local automobile dealership. This type of vehicle was commonly used in Britain as a delivery van, but it was quite roomy inside, and most important of all, it was the least expensive van of its size.

I t took us just one week to outfit the van as a camper. We installed two storage boxes (along the side walls) that doubled as benches, a collapsible table, a standing closet for our one good set of clothing each and a food cupboard that we fashioned from a small, wooden army case. If I do say so myself, the bed was an ingenious design. When we collapsed the table and fitted it between the two storage boxes, a double bed was created. The interior walls and ceiling were insulated with Styrofoam to prevent condensation and to keep the van cool during the day and warm at night. Hardboard paneling was installed over the insulation on the interior side walls to provide a more finished appearance. Jean added a homey touch by fashioning cheerfully coloured covers for the foam-filled bench seats (that doubled as a mattress), as well as matching drapes for the rear windows. Another drape of the same material was installed so that at night it could be drawn to separate the cab area from the living section in the rear of the van. Finally, we fitted a carpet over the exposed, metal floor to reduce rattles and road noise. In the end, we had made our camper comfortable and quite cosy. Since we had scavenged many of the materials from around Jean's parents' home, the total cost of outfitting the van was only about 25 pounds sterling.

Our maiden "voyage" was a one-week tour of Scotland to try out the camper. Leaving the village of Rumford, we travelled north and west through Calendar, then alongside Loch Lomond and on to Inverness and the famous Loch Ness (home of Nessie, the Loch Ness monster) in the northern Highlands. We then proceeded east and south to Aberdeen and Dundee. As luck would have it, on the second day out, a large rock was thrown up from the wheels of a passing transport truck, shattering our windshield; it took two days to order and install the new part.

It was fitting that in the somber valley of Glencoe, the site of the massacre of the McDonalds, I had my first encounter with the midge, the Scottish version of the blackfly. I will never forget that scene, standing in the early morning drizzle, my face slathered with shaving cream, trying to shave with a straight razor and slapping wildly at clouds of tiny, biting insects. Jean, meanwhile, sat snugly in the rear of the van, watching the performance and having a good laugh at my predicament.

Following our circular tour of Scotland, we returned to Rumford to say our goodbyes to the family before setting off on the first true leg of our great adventure.

Stirling Castle, in the Central Region, as viewed from the former royal gardens

Church in the remote Moidart area of Scotland

Glen Dochart, in the Central Region, near the road to Crainlarich and Glen Coe

Badentarbat Bay and the Summer Isles of western Scotland

Victoria Falls in the Slattadale Forest on the shores of Loch Maree in Wester Ross

Kilchurn Castle, on an island on Loch Awe in the Strathclyde region, is the ancient seat of the Campbell Clan

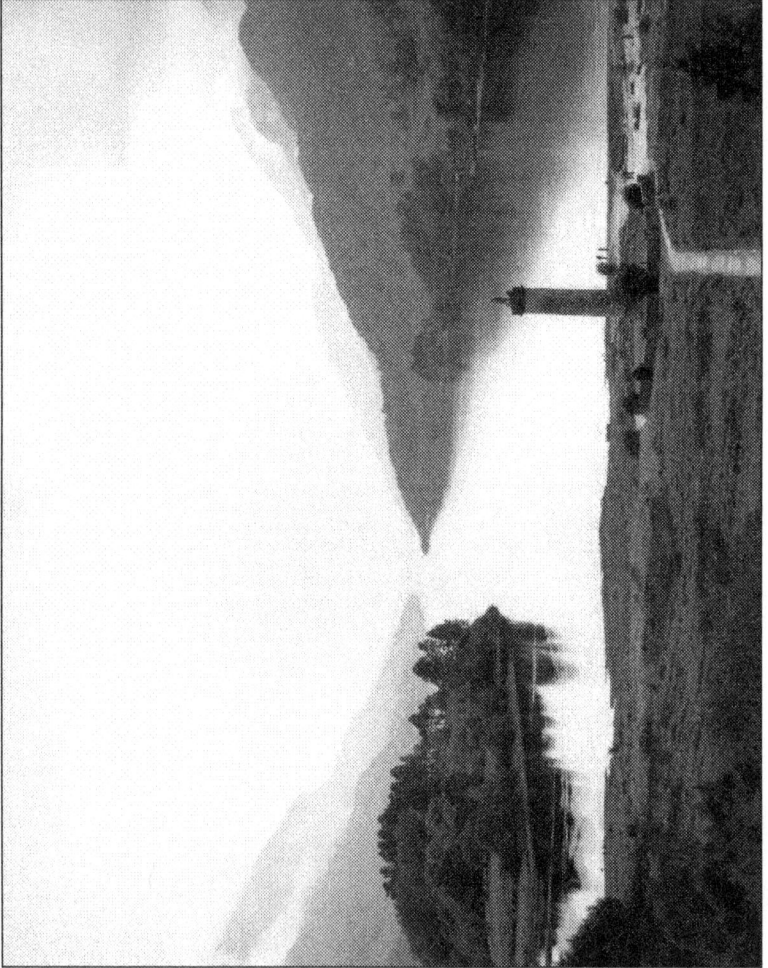

Glenfinnan Monument at the head of Loch Shiel

Deciduous woodland in Glen Lyon in the Tayside region

Taking our time, it took three days to reach Dover, just south of London, where we boarded a ferry for the port of Calais in France. Halfway across the English Channel the clouds parted, and the sun finally appeared. During our month in Britain it had rained every day, and so our overriding thought was to reach the sunny climes of the Mediterranean. Consequently, after landing at Calais, we travelled briskly in a southerly direction through France, passing through Tours, Lemans and Bordeaux.

We entered Spain at San Sebastian on the Bay of Biscay. Before they would allow us to enter the country, the Spanish customs officials required proof that our van was insured. While in Britain, we had inquired about purchasing vehicle insurance in advance for all of the countries in which we planned to travel, but found this was not possible. Insurance could be bought at most border crossings; however, on entry to Spain we were expected to pay for an entire year's coverage. At first, we experienced some difficulty explaining that we only wanted to purchase insurance for one month, the amount of time we expected to be in Spain. Eventually, after a great deal of discussion with customs, we were able to buy one month's vehicle insurance and were permitted to enter the country.

In Britain, I had found driving on the left-hand side of the road a difficult adjustment to make, since in Canada we drove on the right. It was a great relief, therefore, to be back on the right once again, and this was particularly important because now I had to deal with, what we perceived to be, the "mad" driving of the French and Spanish. We were convinced these people had a death wish; the speed at which they drove, and the apparent disregard for life and limb was unbelievable to us.

There were many campgrounds throughout Spain, many of which had outlets for electric razors, shower facilities and small grocery shops. However, for someone from a northern climate, accustomed to hot-water showers, the cold water of the campgrounds provided a shocking start to the day.

We journeyed along the north coast of Spain as far as San Vicente de Barqueret and then turned inland, climbing through the Cantabrian Mountains. The scenery of northern Spain was magnificent. The many shades of lush, green vegetation contrasted sharply with the white walls and orange, clay roofs of the houses that dotted the hillsides.

W E E K 6 S I X ...

It was mid August when we traversed the plains of central Spain where it was hot, dry and dusty. As we travelled through this region, we noticed that much of the farming still relied on traditional methods. The primary source of transportation on the farm appeared to be the donkey- or burro-pulled cart, and it was commonplace to see these vehicles, heavily laden with people and produce, on the roads. During the grain harvest, many farmers still cut their crop, spread it on the ground and then drove ox- or horse-drawn, wooden sleds over it to thresh the grain. Once separated, the grain and chaff were tossed into the air. The chaff being lighter was blown away by the wind, leaving the separated grain behind. Our overall impression was that the people in the rural areas still led a rather rustic and simple life.

There were few campgrounds along the route from Santander, on the Bay of Biscay, to Madrid. We did, however, discover an excellent campsite at Valladolid, a large town midway between the north coast and Madrid, approximately 150 miles from the capital.

After a refreshing two-day stopover at the campground, spent mainly swimming in the pool and sampling the local food and wine, we proceeded to Madrid where we arranged for the van to be serviced. That service was truly good value. For a change of oil, lubrication and overall examination of the vehicle, the total charge was the equivalent of seven Canadian dollars. In addition, we were given the excess motor oil that had not been used when the oil was changed.

From Madrid, we travelled east to Valencia, then south and southwest along the coast of the Mediterranean Sea, taking about three days to drive the 150 miles to Cartagena. Daytime temperatures rose to about 90 degrees Fahrenheit, so a good part of each day was spent sun bathing and swimming in the sea. During the heat of the afternoon, we would often visit whatever town was nearby to shop for groceries. At the time, it seemed to us that the price of canned goods was relatively high, so our diet consisted largely of fresh fruit and vegetables, as well as the basic bread and butter. I must admit that during the first week or two in Spain I fell into the habit of supping on the local bread and large quantities of red table wine. This habit continued until one day I could no longer bear the thought of downing another glass of that rough, tart liquid. Bread and butter, nevertheless, remained a staple of our diet, partly because *pain y mantiquilla* were among the few Spanish words we knew.

Some of the overnight stops we made along the coast were somewhat disappointing, particularly the towns of Benidorm and Torremolinos. Essentially, they were British holiday enclaves, and the local businesses catered to tourists, supplying everything British right down to the fish and chip shops. In our view, the local character of these towns had been overshadowed by the foreign resort atmosphere.

W E E K   S E V E N ...

After a week of lazy travel down *La Playa Del Sol*, we reached Almeria. There, we found a wonderful campground where we decided to stay for a few days. In the camp supermarket, we purchased snorkels and masks. Eager to get into the water after driving in the heat of the day, Jean quickly changed into her bathing suit and sprinted down the beach into the sea. With a yelp, she retreated just as quickly back to the beach. She had managed to step on a sea urchin. Her introduction to this spiny creature was a memorable one. Scores of painful, black barbs were lodged in the soles of her feet, and the balance of the afternoon was spent drawing out the spines. So much for the swim that day! From that point onward, we were extremely careful about entering and leaving the water, and for the next several days we spent most of our time floating on the surface near the shore, using our snorkeling gear to observe the myriad of colours and shapes of the undersea world.

Too much of a good thing can sometimes lead to discontent. After nearly a month of this lazy life-style in Spain we were becoming restless. Besides, we knew that at some point we would have to work to augment our finances, and so our thoughts began to turn to countries where we might possibly work during the winter. We had heard that German companies often hired foreign labourers, so we began to think seriously about travelling north to Germany.

One afternoon, when we had all but resigned ourselves to spending a winter in Europe, a B. M. W. motorcycle and a Land-Rover with a trailer in tow—packed to the gunnels with jerry cans and all manner of camping gear—roared into camp. It looked and sounded as though a small army had arrived, but in fact, only three people had created the din. Curious as to why anyone vacationing in Spain would require so much equipment, we struck up a conversation with them.

Robin, Phil and Vivian, from Tunbridge Wells, England, told us about their plan to cross the Sahara Desert and then travel south and east through Central Africa to visit an uncle who owned a tea plantation on the slopes of Mount Elgon in Kenya. Being of similar age and background, we immediately hit it off with the Britons, and a few hours later, they invited us to travel with them provided we could obtain the necessary visas for several North- and Central-African countries. This left us in a real quandary. Adventure was one thing, but the overland journey across Africa sounded risky. Would our van be able to withstand the beating it would surely take on rough roads? Could we acquire the necessary visas on such short notice? Were we actually willing to potentially risk our lives? The option of a winter in Germany, although not as exciting, seemed a more safe and sane alternative.

After a restless night and much anxious thought, however, we finally decided to put a little zest into our lives and opt for the great African adventure. On the morning of September 3rd, we arranged our rendezvous site, a campground in the centre of Tangier, Morocco, where we would meet the trio two weeks hence. Having committed ourselves to the overland trek, we set off for North Africa to make the necessary arrangements.

.

Preparing for Travel
in Africa

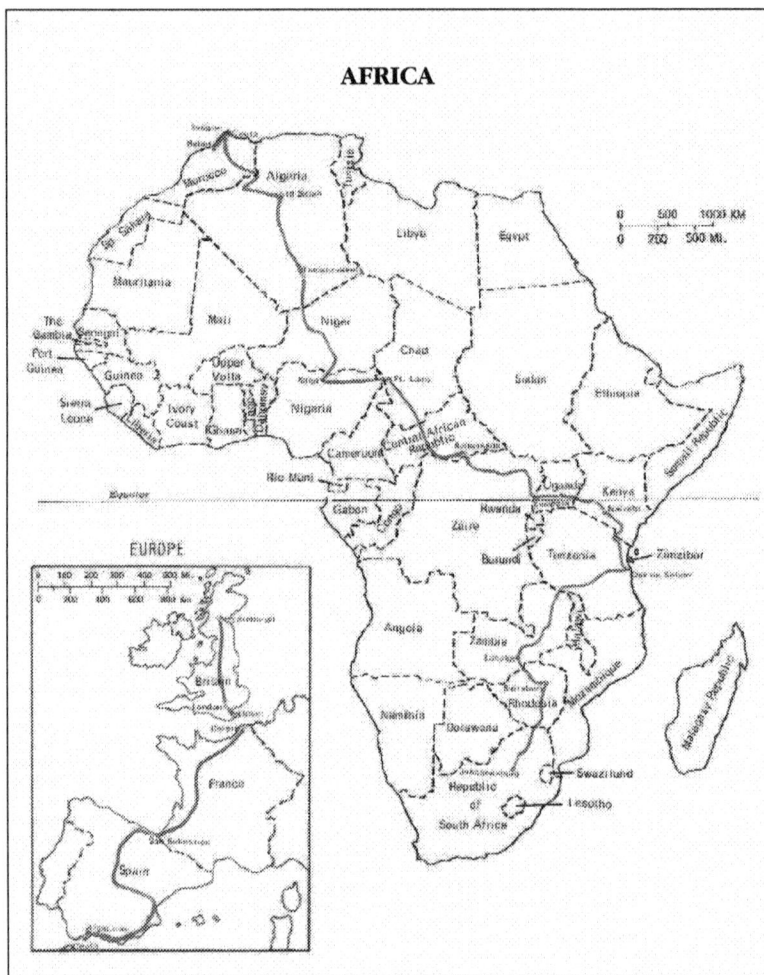

AFRICA

EUROPE

After we parted company with our newly found friends, our overriding concern was how much we had to do in so little time. We hastened to Algeciras and caught the daily ferryboat for the two-hour journey to Ceuta, Morocco. It was a glorious, sunny day as we sailed out of the harbour at Algeciras, and from the sea, a panoramic view of the Rock of Gibraltar awaited us. Calm were the waters as we voyaged across the Strait of Gibraltar, and the quiet sea, combined with the constant throbbing of the ship's engines, began to lull us into a state of relaxation and tranquillity. But soon, as the coast of North Africa loomed larger, our pulses quickened at the thought of our impending adventures in unknown Africa.

Immediately after disembarking, we cleared customs on the outskirts of Ceuta, and right away, as we began to drive in Morocco, the feeling of high adventure seized us. The people looked so different. The women wore long, black robes, and their faces were hidden by yashmaks; the men wore caftans; and there were camels kneeling on the sandy beach. Any doubts we may have had about the proposed expedition were dispelled by the lure of Arab Africa.

Soon after our arrival in Tangier, we learned that all of our visas would have to be obtained at the various embassies in Morocco's capital city, Rabat, located about 150 miles south of Tangier on the country's west coast. We hurried on to Rabat, realizing that we only had about ten days to arrange visas for Algeria, Cameroon, Chad, Central African Republic and the Congo Republic, as well as make all of the other preparations for the African journey.

Cameroon, Chad and Central African Republic were former French colonies, and as such, were represented in Rabat by the French Embassy which refused to issue us visas without a *Letter of Introduction.* Since there was no Canadian Embassy in Morocco, the British Embassy provided services to nationals of Commonwealth countries that were not locally represented. The Moroccan in charge of inquiries at the British Embassy insisted he was not authorized to supply us a *Letter of Introduction* because we were not residents of Morocco. Frustrated, we asked for an appointment with the Ambassador, only to be told we couldn't see him for at least a week. After much shuttling back and forth between the British and French Consulates, getting nowhere and accomplishing nothing, we were at our wits' end.

In desperation, we decided to telephone the nearest Canadian Embassy which was located in Madrid. Long-distance telephone calls could be made from the central post office in Rabat, but they had to be booked in advance. Eventually, after a two-hour wait for the connection to be made, we were actually speaking to a Canadian, in fact, the Canadian Ambassador himself. After a brief conversation in which we outlined our problem, he told us to present ourselves at the French Embassy one hour hence and our needs would be met. True to his word, the Ambassador must have immediately contacted the French Embassy, because upon our arrival a short time later we found that all three visas had been prepared.

By this time, nearly a week had elapsed since we had left our new friends. We now had visas for three countries, and obtaining the other two was relatively straightforward, involving only minor irritations for us. For instance, at the Congolese Embassy, while being interviewed by the Ambassador, he insisted on speaking in French only, even though he could speak English well. Our facility with the

French language was very limited; nevertheless, his reaction to our difficulty was simply to say in English, "if you can't understand, that's your problem not mine!"After several hours, though, we did receive the visas. At the Algerian Embassy, we were initially told our visas would be prepared for us in a few days' time. After much pleading and our continual presence in the Embassy halls during the day, we received our visas in two days.

Another type of documentation that we attempted to acquire was a *Carnet de Passage*. Essentially, this was a customs document for the vehicle that guaranteed the owner would not sell it without paying a country's import duty. Usually, this document was obtained through an automobile club such as the Ontario Motor League in Canada. The auto club issued the *Carnet* once the owners had frozen a required sum of money in their bank account and had given the club access to those funds if the vehicle was sold illegally in a foreign country. In that event, the auto club could be held responsible for the duty. Although many countries (notably European) did not require such documentation, a *Carnet de Passage* was required by some. I strongly recommend that anyone travelling extensively by vehicle consider obtaining a *Carnet* or its equivalent, as one could be denied entry to a country or be required to deposit large sums of money with customs. In such cases, the funds are usually returned upon exit from the country, but this can lead to a variety of problems (some of which we encountered and which are described later). Unfortunately, we were unable to obtain this document in Morocco, and because of the length of time it would have taken to arrange documentation from Canada, we elected to take our chances without a *Carnet de Passage*.

Our first impression of Rabat was that it appeared to be a modern capital city, but the sanitary conditions left much to be desired. It was commonplace, while driving along the coastal road, to see men urinating and defecating in public. The toilet facilities, even in many of the best restaurants, were primitive by western standards. Commonly, there was a hole in the ground for defecation and urination; a wooden spatula was available in lieu of toilet tissue; and a tin can, filled with water, was provided for hand washing.

After completing our business in Rabat, we returned once again to Tangier. We still had three days before the arrival of our friends, so we used the time to make a few purchases for the up-coming journey. We bought a forty-five gallon drum to store gasoline, for we knew there would be long stretches in remote areas where there would be no fuel depots. This drum, combined with the van's tank (eight gallons), gave us a total range of nearly 1,200 miles. Anticipating hot, dry conditions and few water sources on the desert crossing, we purchased two plastic water containers with a combined capacity of eighteen gallons and salt tablets to help retain water in our bodies. Even though the van's tires were tubeless, we carried spare inner tubes that could be inflated inside the tires with a foot pump in the event of blowouts. In addition, the Scottish dealership where we had purchased the vehicle had provided us with an extra fan belt and various other spare parts such as fuses. Realizing that mosquitoes could be a problem south of the Sahara, we also bought malaria pills and mosquito netting.

We had heard that Michelin produced detailed maps including information such as locations of water wells, gasoline depots and road conditions in all seasons, so we purchased a series of these maps for our intended route as far as Kenya. We carried 500 dollars in Canadian and American small bills, as well as 500 hundred dollars in traveller's cheques, and we maintained a reserve fund in our Canadian account to which we could wire for money in emergencies. For nourishment

Typical brass and copper shop in the kasbah, Tangier

we purchased rice, coffee, dehydrated foods such as curries and milk, tinned goods such as sardines and fruit and a large store of fresh fruits and vegetables.

In hindsight, our preparations were rather scant. On a journey like this a comprehensive vehicle repair manual, a complete tool kit, a wider variety of spare parts and a good working knowledge of the vehicle are recommended.

During the evenings that remained before our friends' arrival, we visited the kasbah and other points of interest in Tangier. The number of people peddling hashish and marijuana on the streets was an eye-opener for us, and on many occasions we were solicited to buy illicit drugs; street urchins constantly harassed us with cries of, *"donnez-moi un cadeau"* (give me a gift); beggars seemed to be on every street corner; and on the beach below our campsite, the local inhabitants were quarantined due to a recent outbreak of cholera.

The Saharan Adventure Unfolds

.

On the afternoon of September 13th, we arrived back in camp after shopping to find that Robin, Phil and Vivian had arrived, a little ahead of schedule. They were still very eager to have us join them on the trip, so the next day we all went on a shopping expedition to pick up the remaining odds and ends we needed. Robin was well-read on the subject of travelling in Africa. He carried a collection of books by explorers and adventurers such as Schweitzer, Lawrence and Thesiger, from whose accounts I am convinced he got the idea of wearing a flowing, white Arab robe, or thobe, which became his manner of dress for the entire desert crossing.

Tree-lined river valley in the Atlas Mountains

The hot, dry ascent through the Atlas Mountains

At any rate, on the 15th, we departed from Tangier, travelling inland in a southeasterly direction, and as we neared the Atlas Mountains, we began to climb. This part of Morocco was hot, dry and desolate; consequently, the only pockets of vegetation were near the water sources—along the river margins and at oases where there were springs and wells.

From time to time during the first day of our journey, we encountered groups of children from local villages who stood at the side of the road, entreating motorists to buy fruits and vegetables from them. In some cases, they even tried to sell live lizards which they held aloft by their tails. We had no idea whether the lizards were meant to be food or pets, but in any case, we restricted our purchases to fruit, particularly pomegranates. Most often, the children wanted money for their wares, but in some instances they were anxious to trade for items such as paper and pencils which were rare luxury items for them.

Typical, centuries-old Moroccan town

On the second day out, we were struck by a sudden, violent hail storm as we climbed through the mountains. One minute it was hot and dry under a brilliant, blue sky, the next, an icy wind freshened, the sky blackened and hail began to batter against the van. For once, we did not envy Robin and Viv in the open Land-Rover, or Phil on his motorcycle. Fortunately, the freak storm passed quickly, leaving us shaken but having caused no damage.

Approximately 150 miles south of Tangier we were faced with a choice of roads leading to Algeria and the Sahara. One road was paved highway but meant a lengthy detour. The other was a more direct route but was unpaved. Our friends advocated the shorter alternative because they were confident their vehicles could negotiate rough terrain; with some trepidation, we agreed on the more direct route. It wasn't long, though, before we wished we were back on paved highway. As we had feared, our progress was slowed by deep sand that had drifted over the path in some areas,

Mountain oasis thick with date palms

and by rocky sections in others where we were afraid of damaging the tires and underside of the van.

Just before sunset, we pulled off the track at the site of a rocky outcrop that looked like it would make a good, sheltered campsite. No sooner had we stopped our vehicles when an Arab suddenly appeared and asked if he and his family could camp beside us that night. Cautious and concerned about the possibility of being robbed, we attempted to explain to him that we preferred to camp alone; however, undaunted the man ran off, purportedly to fetch his family. The moment he was out of sight, we restarted our engines and drove off hurriedly in search of another campsite. Many times over the next several months we would remark upon how extraordinary it was that even in what appeared to be the most isolated, seemingly deserted regions, the moment we stopped, people would appear as if by magic.

After another hard day's travel, we arrived at Beni-Ounif,

Tiny Algerian oasis, too small to support settlement

a small town on the Morocco-Algeria border, where paved highway resumed. We still had a few Moroccan dhirahms and francs, so before crossing into Algeria we decided to buy some grapes and watermelons to use up the Moroccan currency. At the border post, the Algerian officials asked if we carried any food purchased in Morocco, and if so, to either eat or discard it before entering the country. We were also ordered to empty all of our water containers. Apparently, these measures were deemed necessary because of the cholera outbreak in Tangier. We pleaded to save our canned goods, arguing that they were sealed and couldn't possibly carry disease, but our entreaties were to no avail. Now, we were faced with a dilemma. We had bought a large quantity of tinned food in Morocco; what were we to do with it? Phil, determined not to waste the food, promptly sat at the side of the road and began to wolf down sardines, but after the eighth can, he had to give up. It was impossible to consume all of our food stores at one sitting, so we became resigned to leaving some at the roadside.

In a fit of temper, Robin grabbed his machete and began smashing and chopping a watermelon. Seeing this, the Algerian border police were furious and ordered him to desist immediately. (In that part of the world, food was synonymous with survival, and its waste or destruction was considered criminal.) Robin was advised that he would only be allowed into the country if he gathered up all of the discarded food and donated it to the people of Beni-Ounif. He was also ordered to apologize to both the Moroccan and Algerian border officials. For the longest time he stubbornly refused, but eventually, realizing that his great adventure was in jeopardy, he swallowed his pride and complied with the orders.

This, however, was not the end of our difficulties entering Algeria. About two miles further on, we were directed to stop at a second customs post where, convinced we were carrying drugs, the officers proceeded to search our vehicles thoroughly. (This was at a time when many young Europeans and North Americans had been arrested and jailed for drug possession.) The search lasted nearly two hours, and finding nothing illegal, they ushered us into an office for questioning. For another hour we stood at a counter completing forms and answering questions. Suddenly, Phil tugged gently on Vivian's arm and pointed downward. There, resting on his foot, partially hidden under a trouser leg, was a can of sardines. Without telling anyone, Phil had decided to hide a few cans in his clothing, and now one of them had fallen down his pant leg onto his foot. Luckily, the customs officers hadn't noticed this, but they looked up quickly when Jean and Viv began to snicker. When asked why they were laughing, the girls replied that it was just a humorous story they had remembered; fortunately, customs did not pursue this further. At the first opportunity, Phil surreptitiously slipped the sardine can into his pocket, and not long afterward we were permitted to enter Algeria. It was fortunate for us all that Phil had not been caught in the act of smuggling food.

Later that day, however, safe in camp, everyone confessed to having done much the same thing as Phil. For instance, Robin and Viv had hidden tins of powdered milk under the hood of the Land-Rover, and Jean and I had transferred food in Moroccan packages to containers with European labels.

The customs clearance had taken so long that we merely drove to the outskirts of town where we made camp by the side of the road. Just as we began to prepare the evening meal, flute and drum music and an occasional, eerie, high-pitched wailing sound floated over the otherwie-still night air.

Out of curiosity, I wandered back into town to discover the origin of the unusual sounds. One of the first people I encountered, a young boy, explained that a wedding ceremony was underway in a nearby village, and asked if we would like to attend. Naturally, when I took this invitation back to the group, they were all anxious to witness such a celebration, so we decided to follow the lad. As he struck off into the desert, we followed, but as the flickering lights of town disappeared behind us, and we became enveloped in darkness, our level of apprehension rose. Would we be attacked and robbed? Or worse? I must admit to feeling particularly uneasy because around my waist in a money belt, I carried all of our cash and traveller's cheques, about 1,000 dollars.

Several minutes later, with the music becoming progressively louder, we reached a village and proceeded to wind our way through narrow, dark alleyways. All at once, our worries evaporated as we entered a square courtyard that presented a scene that was straight out of "Arabian Nights." Men were seated on three sides of the courtyard that was open to the sky; the fourth side was occupied by an orchestra and the male contingent of the wedding party. In the centre of the yard, young boys and men gyrated to the beat of the music. Gayly coloured carpets hung from a second-

Ancient, walled desert town

floor balcony overlooking the courtyard, and peering over the balcony were the village women, veiled and cloaked in white. It was they who had produced the high-pitched, wailing sound (ululations) we had heard as they trilled in unison at strategic points in the music.

Our guide introduced us to the father of the groom who immediately called for the music to be stopped, and announced to all assembled that we were honoured wedding guests. (Apparently, our arrival was considered a good-luck omen for the newlyweds.) We were invited to sit among the men on the margin of the dance floor, and once seated were served mint tea. Since they were not Arabic, Jean and Vivian were permitted to sit among the men, and this was most unusual since women were generally barred from mingling with men on such occasions.

A group of males, sporting colourful scarfs and pretending to be women, danced in front of the bridegroom, and it wasn't long before they asked me to dance. We speculated later that they probably found my long, blond hair attractive. Of course Jean and our friends were anxious to see me get up and make a fool of myself, so they prodded and pleaded until I finally agreed. The men wanted to see me dance the twist, so I went at it, twisting the night away amid the cheering, clapping and whistling of the crowd. After several numbers, with a great sense of relief, I was able to excuse myself from the dance floor. Do you think I could talk my companions into dancing? Not a chance!

Following some toasts and speech making, our host led us to a small room where we were served supper. He explained that wedding celebrations normally lasted about a week. On the first day, the meal was very simple, and each day that followed, a greater variety of food was added. This being the first day of the wedding festivities, only plain cous-cous (a North African dish of steamed, granulated wheat) and mint tea were served. The meal finished, we thanked our host, and one of the customs officials who had given us such a hard time earlier that day, kindly offered to lead us back to our camp. We were thrilled to have been given the opportunity of experiencing an aspect of local life unavailable to most tourists.

The next day, we proceeded south to the town of Bechar which marked the end of the paved highway. Four or five miles from town, we spotted an island of vegetation not far from the road and decided to camp there for the weekend.

Reaching this small oasis, we found a tiny, one-room adobe building concealed in a coppice of reeds. Inside this dwelling lived an old man who claimed to be seventy-five years of age. His was a Spartan existence. In the centre of the concrete floor was his cooking fire, and he shared the single, unadorned room with his small flock of goats. The old man was delighted to have our company, and over the course of the weekend we had many interesting conversa-

Our encampment at the small oasis near Bechar

tions with him. Like all of the Arabs we met, this person made us feel welcome with offerings of mint tea. At the end of the weekend we bade the old man goodbye and took his photograph. When we asked how we could send him a copy, the only address he knew for himself was "*Grande Sahara.*"

That Monday morning in Bechar was spent changing more dollars into Algerian currency, replenishing our gas tanks, buying food and purchasing an oil-bath air filter for our van. We had been under the misconception that our vehicle was equipped with an oil-bath filter, but to our consternation, we found that a paper filter was standard equipment in an Austin-Morris van. Everyone we spoke to advised us that a paper filter would not be effective in the sandy, dusty environment of the desert, so we made the necessary conversion. However, because the oil-bath filter remained attached to the original filter, the added strain on the engine drastically reduced our gas mileage.

The old Algerian we met near Bechar

On leaving Bechar, Robin allowed Vivian to drive the Land-Rover for the first time. All went well for several miles, then suddenly, the vehicle veered off the road, overturning the trailer. When we arrived on the scene, gasoline had spilled on the road, suitcases had burst open and clothes were strewn everywhere. Phil, riding immediately behind the Land-Rover, had been treated to the spectacle of their gear flying off the trailer in all directions as it jack-knifed across the road. It took some time to collect the stray articles of clothing, and I will always remember the scene of Phil, chasing Vivian's elusive, wind-blown underwear, and wailing that he'd have to chase her knickers all over Africa.

Back on the road again a short while later, we had our first sight of sand dunes. The impression many people have of the desert is that it is a sea of rolling dunes. Generally, though, this was not the case on the route we followed across the Sahara. On the entire desert crossing, we encountered sand dunes on only three or four occasions. Seeing the great dunes for the first time, the three men, pretending to be Lawrence of Arabia, scrambled to the summit of the highest mound.

The paved highway ended where the dunes began. For the next 1,000 miles, we would make our way along sandy or rocky trails, sometimes marked but often not. Many stretches of road were indiscernible, but whenever this occurred, the path was usually marked by empty oil drums, metal stakes or mounds of stones placed at regular intervals.

We set out in an easterly direction on a sandy track marked by occasional piles of stones. This roadway eventually inter-

Cooking over a dung-fuelled fire

sected with another which followed an ancient camel-caravan route between Algiers on the Mediterranean Sea coast and Kano in northern Nigeria. The distance from Bechar to the north-south caravan route was about 300 miles over relatively flat, sandy terrain, dotted with occasional oases.

Earlier that day, in Bechar, we had purchased a leg of goat meat for our evening meal, so late that afternoon we began to look for a suitable campsite with a source of firewood. Eventually, we glimpsed a solitary tree on the horizon far from the road and decided to stop there for the night. Machetes in hand, we attempted to hack small branches from the tree, but we were unsuccessful; the tree was just too tough. In desperation, we hitched the Land-Rover to a branch using a strong, nylon rope, but still the tree refused to yield us any wood.

Just as we were about to give up on the idea of a fire, I remembered a geography lesson in which I had learned that in many countries where wood was scarce, the people used

Stuck again—almost a daily occurrence on the Sahara

dried manure as fuel. Fortunately, there was an abundance of animal droppings all over the area, so buckets in hand, we set about collecting camel dung. I can still hear Phil, in his very proper English accent, wailing, "to think I came all the way to Africa just to pick up camel shit!" We must have made quite a sight, the five of us scooping up and testing Saharan road apples to be sure they were dry, but it worked. With a little paper in the centre of the pile, the fire started easily, and the dung burned just like charcoal. Jean was adamant that she wasn't going to eat the meat if it was exposed to the smoke from the fire, so we covered the meat with tin foil. In the end, the meal was delicious, and we all had a sense of pride at having been so resourceful.

The following morning, before setting out on the day's journey, Robin, Phil and I decided to try to adjust the van's oil-bath filter in an attempt to reduce gasoline consumption. To our surprise, a few moments into the operation, we heard the roar of an approaching transport truck that sud-

Police station in Reggane (note the signs in French and Arabic)

denly bounded off the road and ploughed across the desert toward us. In a cloud of dust, the driver brought his vehicle to an abrupt halt beside us and asked whether he and his companion could be of any assistance. As we explained what we were trying to do with the filter, Robin offered the strangers cigarettes, which they readily accepted. In return, they brought out a large basket of dates for us, and proceeded to take charge of the work on the filter. As we parted company a short while later, the two men supplied us with mint leaves so we could make our own tea en route. We were to find that this sort of friendliness and willingness to help strangers would be commonplace as we traversed the continent over the next several months.

That day, we learned how treacherous sand could be. One minute, the sandy track would be hard-packed like asphalt; the next, it would be soft and unable to bear the weight of the vehicles. In sandy stretches, we kept our eyes glued to the road ahead, desperately trying to anticipate the condition

Roadside well constructed of dried mud and wooden poles

of the sand. Frequently, we drove off the track to avoid becoming mired, and on these occasions, all three vehicles would forge their own trails parallel to the main road. Phil had developed a habit of disappearing alone on little side trips, and on one of these lone sojourns, managed to become stuck; he was unable to dislodge the heavy motorbike from the deep, loose sand. That episode was costly in terms of lost travel time spent looking for him, not to mention the needless consumption of valuable gasoline. After eight gruelling hours of driving, becoming stuck and digging ourselves out of sand, time and again, we arrived in Reggane just as the sun was setting. We proceeded directly to the local *gendarmerie* to ask if we could camp in the police compound that night, but before answering our question, they responded with one of their own. "May we see your travel papers?" Travel papers?! We had no idea what they were talking about. We were to learn that all travellers crossing the Algerian desert were required to report to every police station on their

Well in Oulef (note the dried-mud construction)

itinerary, to record their names, the next town on their route and their estimated time of arrival. This regulation was meant to protect travellers, for in theory, the police radioed travel plans to the next station, and if the travellers did not arrive as scheduled, a search party was organized. The importance of the regulation became clear when we learned about the recent death of three Frenchmen who had also attempted to cross the desert. Apparently, they had become lost in an area where the trail was unmarked and had perished when their supplies of gasoline and water had become exhausted. When their bodies were discovered, it must have been a gruesome sight; two were found entombed in their car; the third was located some distance away, his flesh eaten away by birds and insects.

We asked the police in Reggane to issue travel documents and to provide us with the appropriate, official stamps to indicate we had reached the town safely. Unfortunately, the small-town bureaucrats refused to cooperate, insisting that

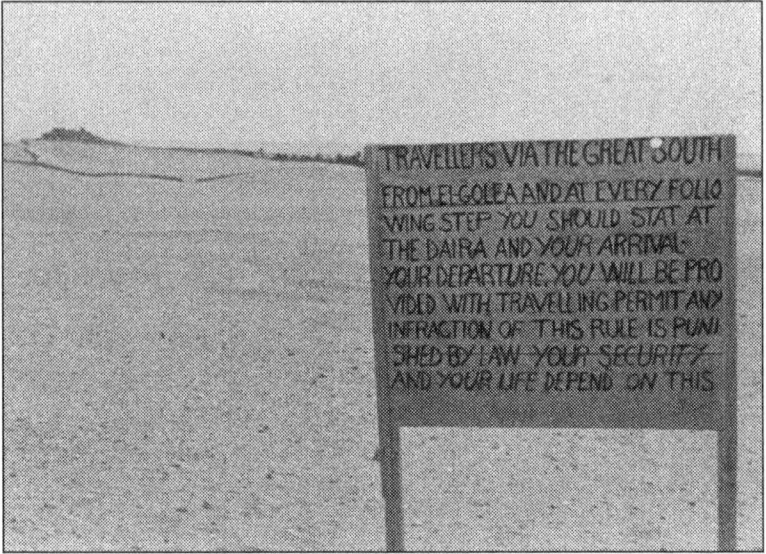

Warning notice to Sahara travellers

we return to Bechar for the initial paperwork. Our spirits plummeted at the thought of having to re-experience the last stretch of desert not just once, but two more times. After a short conference, the four of us agreed that it would be too painful to turn back, and we promptly drove out of town in an easterly direction. With several miles behind us, we stopped for the night, feeling relatively confident the police were unaware of our decision to carry on "illegally."

The next day, we followed the stone markers, where they were visible, and relied on compass bearings when we were unable to discern where the road lay. Eventually, we caught sight of the village of Oulef, and it was on the approach to this community that we discovered a signpost, in broken English, that finally described the desert-travel regulations. In Oulef, we tried once again to obtain travel documents from the *gendarmes*. This time, the village police were exceedingly friendly, offering us rooms in the station, but we elected to camp outside in their compound. Jean and

The marketplace of In Salah

Vivian were especially popular with the policemen as they had few opportunities to see women in the village. (The local women were not often allowed out of their homes, and when they were, they were always veiled.) Jean and Viv were attractive, young women, but being from the West, the local men found them to be positively exotic, and this was especially so when the girls wore skimpy tops and shorts. At any rate, we certainly received every attention and service from the police in Oulef. Unable to issue us with the proper travel documents, they nevertheless promised to radio ahead to the next town, In Salah, to arrange to have documentation prepared for us on our arrival.

With business attended to, the policemen and an Egyptian agricultural researcher (who was studying methods of cultivating tomatoes in the desert) went out of their way to give us a tour of the community. The village's wells were fed by an underground stream that was inhabited by small fish. Well water was raised in two ways. Some wells relied on a buck-

Early morning preparations in In Salah

et-and-pulley system; others—step wells—had stairways
leading to an underground stream where buckets were used
to scoop up water.

The following morning, we bade farewell to our friends in
Oulef and headed eastward to In Salah. The journey was not
difficult, except when we tried to find the track into town. In
Salah, we were to discover, was completely surrounded by
gigantic sand dunes, and there was only one trail in and out
of town. Upon entering the oasis, we noticed that water
abounded and the many date palms were lush and laden
with fruit. Robin, our law student, seeing the dates hanging
in great bunches at the roadside, quickly brought the Land-
Rover to a halt; he simply couldn't resist liberating a few
dates.

The balance of the day was spent first acquiring our travel papers, then exploring In Salah. (True to their word, the
police in Oulef had arranged for the documents to be prepared for our arrival.) The marketplace was an intriguing

Corrugated road in central Algeria

feature of the town. Most of the town's consumer goods were supplied by means of transport trucks that made regular visits to the larger desert settlements. Flour, for the baking of bread, was a common item brought in by truck, but supplies were limited. As a result, a fixed amount of bread was available for sale each day. Since there was seldom an oversupply of food, most of it was sold soon after the market opened, and by noon there was virtually nothing left to buy. Consequently, the vendors generally spent the afternoon resting or engaging in desultory conversation in shady corners of the market square.

Rising early in the morning to take advantage of the coolest part of the day for driving was becoming our habit, since by ten or eleven, temperatures were scorching. At five the next morning, therefore, we prepared for departure from In Salah. To our surprise, many of the town's children, who obviously had not been exposed to many foreigners, ringed our campsite to observe the *"touristes;"* Phil's motorbike

The boulder field in central Algeria

always created the greatest amount of interest.

The southbound route to Tamanrasset was a road in name only; actually, it was little more than a corrugated, rocky trail. There were two prevailing theories about how one should travel over washboard. Some people were of the opinion it was better to speed over the corrugations, in a sense "floating" over the tops of the bumps; others maintained it was better to drive slowly. Our friends opted for speed whereas we believed our van would fare better at a slower pace. As a result, Jean and I advanced painfully slowly, felt every bump in the road but experienced no serious problems. The others, however, were less fortunate. Because of the hard pounding, the trailer's springs broke, and eventually, it was abandoned when we reached Tamanrasset. The motorcycle punctured two tires on the rough roads, and in fact, Phil was a very lucky young man. Both blowouts occurred while he was driving at high speed, and on one occasion he narrowly missed smashing his head against a rocky outcrop.

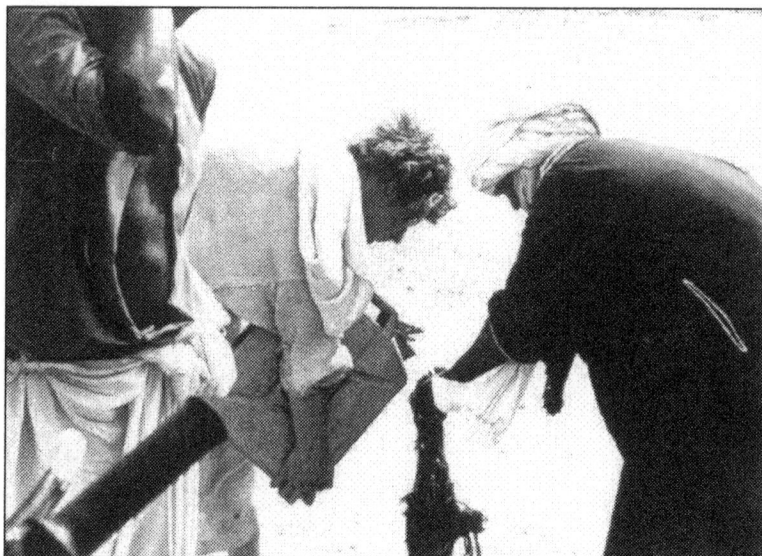

Filling a Touareg's goatskin bag with water

Phil had only carried two spare inner tubes, and now that both were gone, we seriously considered dismantling the bike and transporting it in pieces to Tamanrasset. But providence smiled upon Phil once again; within minutes of his last accident, a large transport truck, travelling in the opposite direction, arrived on the scene. Coincidentally, it was carrying a motorcycle with tires the same size as Phil's. The motorcycle's owner obligingly donated two inner tubes to see Phil through to the next large town.

Mobile once again, we found that just north of Tamanrasset, several miles of road passed through what could only be described as a boulder field. Here, we picked our way across the terrain with extreme care to save the underside of our vehicles from damage. On this boulder field, we encountered two men travelling north in a Volkswagen van. Their gasoline tank had been punctured on the rocks, but they had made temporary repairs, and when we met them they were attempting to buy gasoline from other travellers so

Greatly eroded Ahaggar Mountain Range

they could continue their journey northward to the Mediterranean Sea coast. Unable to convince them to accompany us back to Tamanrasset for help, we gave them a few gallons of gasoline and carried on. During the days and weeks that followed, we wondered what became of the pair.

I mentioned previously that the north-south track we followed down the length of Algeria was an ancient camel-caravan route, and it was fascinating to discover that even at the time of our trip, caravans continued to traverse the desert. One caravan we encountered was low on water, so we replenished the goatskin gourds in which they carried their water supplies.

On our approach to Tamanrasset, we entered the Ahaggar Mountain Range, a series of low mountains which had been greatly eroded over the millennia. It is said that the Saharan sands originated with the mountain ranges, and there was much evidence to support this theory. Huge piles of rubble could be seen at the base of rocky cliffs, and one could imag-

Our typical camp configuration on the desert

ine these rock piles being further eroded by wind, water and temperature fluctuations to eventually produce the desert sand.

As we travelled, we had no idea whether or not there was any need to fear the local inhabitants or animals; however, as a precaution, we normally camped in a square for protection. Although in most instances there proved to be no cause for concern, we learned by experience that there were some potentially dangerous creatures in the desert. For instance, Jean and I had become accustomed to sleeping with the rear doors of the van wide open to take advantage of the cool night air. One night, as she glanced out the back of the van, Jean thought she glimpsed the shape of a dog passing by. Upon investigation in the morning, much to our surprise, we found the paw prints of a mountain lion that had ventured to within just a few feet of our sleeping area. Another potentially dangerous indigenous creature was the scorpion with its poisonous, barbed tail. Usually, the scorpion sting is not lethal to humans unless they are already weakened by age or illness. Nevertheless, the inhabitants of a town just north of Tamanrasset told us that some months prior to our arrival, a foreign traveller had succumbed to the sting of a scorpion that had crawled into his sleeping bag.

WEEK TWELVE ...

Tamanrasset, approximately midway on the desert crossing, was a welcome two-week rest stop for us. On the edge of town we found a unique campground offering reed huts for travellers. Although Jean and I, content with our living arrangements, continued to sleep in the van, our three companions opted for the huts which were a welcome change to the tents to which they were accustomed. Our stopover afforded us time to service and repair the vehicles. The rough driving conditions had taken their toll on them, but the greatest problem had been the blowing sand that had seeped into every crack and crevice. As a result, we took a great deal of time and care to clear the brakes and engine parts of the insidious layers of dust and sand.

At this time, Jean suffered from severe stomach cramps, probably due to the poor quality of the water which tasted strongly of sulphur and salt. She had also developed a craving for something other than the dehydrated foods we had been eating for so long. In particular, she yearned for eggs, so I searched all over town for them. In the entire settlement, I was able to find only one egg, a guinea fowl egg at that, but she was well pleased that I had been able to find it, and she delighted in its taste.

Making repairs during our stopover in Tamanrasset

During our stay in "Tam," we met a variety of interesting people of different nationalities and in various circumstances. For example, an American family was attempting to have its truck repaired. The husband was a college professor on sabbatical from a southwestern U.S. university, and he, his wife and two teenage children were making their way to Tanzania, in East Africa, where they planned to climb Mt. Kilimanjaro. They had purchased a Dodge Fargo truck in the United States and had shipped it to Africa thinking this was just the thing for travel on rough roads. Unfortunately, the universal joint had seized, and at the time we met them, they were deciding whether to order the necessary parts from the States (which would have taken weeks), or to have a temporary repair made. They were still in town when we left a few days later.

Another fellow traveller, a Ceylonese doctor, was making his way to Zaria, Nigeria to visit his father who was a lectur-

61

A street scene in Tamanrasset

er at the local university. The doctor was attempting to cross
the Sahara in a thirteen-year-old Volkswagen "Bug" that was
in such poor condition we wondered whether it had any
chance of completing the journey. The accelerator cable had
broken, so he had rigged a length of wire from the engine
through the interior of the car to the driver's position. With
the cable wrapped around his hand as he drove, he was able
to vary his speed by pulling on the wire. He also claimed to
have no visas for any of the African countries through which
he intended to travel nor any insurance on his vehicle.
According to the Ceylonese, he had driven this rattletrap of
a car around the world, subsidized by the Volkswagen company, as a promotional stunt, and he was now capping off
the journey by making the difficult desert crossing.

Another young man, accompanied by his wife and two
young children, was determined to cross the desert in an
old, dilapidated van, and with only 50 dollars in his pocket.
It was inconceivable to us how anyone could place his fam-

ily in such jeopardy. If what he said was true, he didn't even have sufficient funds to buy the gasoline required to reach Nigeria. Everyone in town advised him to return north to the coast.

We also encountered two Australian couples, travelling together in an enormous World War II ambulance. The interior setup they had was incredible, with bunk beds and large storage lockers filled with tinned goods. They told us that when looking for a vehicle for their trip, they had wanted a rugged and powerful machine. What they hadn't considered was that the tremendous weight of the vehicle would cause it to sink in soft sand more easily than a lighter one. Another of the problems they had to endure was the truck's exceedingly low gas mileage (about eight miles to the gallon).

Many scientists believe that at one time the Sahara Desert was the location of a great inland sea, that forests existed on the water margins providing habitats for a great variety of wildlife, and that humans also inhabited the area. During our stay in Tamanrasset, we found some evidence to support this theory. One of the townspeople gave us a piece of petrified wood and some stone arrowheads that he said were found locally, and in the nearby hills, ancient cave paintings depicted a variety of animals such as antelope and elephants, as well as human hunters.

After our sojourn in Tamanrasset we proceeded south toward the border with Niger. En route, we happened upon two lone Arab women who were travelling the desert by donkey. Slung across the saddle in front of one of the women was an infant, wrapped in cloth. When we stopped to converse with them, we were surprised when the woman, presumably the child's mother, merely laid it on the stony ground. Jean noticed that both women wore silver bracelets, and she was anxious to trade for them. She tried to offer several different items in exchange, but the only trade they would make was for our gold wedding rings, which, of course, we insisted on keeping. As we stood haggling, Phil ventured a little too close to the rear end of one of the donkeys, and unceremoniously, it "misbehaved" on his foot. (Now there was a donkey with a good sense of timing and a great sense of humour!) Realizing there would be no trade, the women remounted their animals and rode off northward.

Just outside the Niger border, at the frontier post named Assamaka, there was no road to speak of, just a flat landscape and soft, loose sand as far as the eye could see. As was often the case, we managed to become trapped in the sand. When stuck, our customary procedure was to dig the sand away from the wheels and then place a sand ladder (a length of flat iron) in front of the rear wheels so the van would have something solid to grip. Jean's job was to push while I tried to coax the van onto the sand ladders and then on to firmer ground. (Before I am criticized for having Jean do all the pushing, I have to say in defence that she didn't

Lone Arab women traversing the desert by donkey

have a driver's license and was unaccustomed to driving
with a standard gear shift. I must admit, though, that I was
not unhappy about remaining in the truck.) The only problem with this system was that once the van was moving, I
was reluctant to stop until it was on solid ground. As a
result, more often than not, Jean would end up running at
full tilt, her short legs pumping like pistons, carrying those
cursed sand ladders and trying desperately to catch up with
the van.

Our arrival at the border post brought the total number of
foreign vehicles there to seven. Besides the Ceylonese doctor in his Volkswagen "Bug" and the five of us with our three
vehicles, there were two Volkswagen vans, one carrying a
pair of young Czechoslovakian men and the other transporting three middle-aged Germans of whom I became quite
envious. On our desert travels it had been impossible to find
water with a decent taste, let alone flavoured soft drinks.
These three had a large cooler filled with bottles of beer

View of a small Algerian desert settlement

which they ceremoniously drank while the rest of us covetously watched and licked our lips. Finally, there was a French diplomat, driving a Peugeot, who was making his way to Cameroon to work for the Government of France in some capacity.

Each of these groups of people had been travelling independently but had decided to remain at the border post for a few days to await the arrival of a guide who would lead them across the next 300 miles, an extremely dangerous stretch of desert; in many places there would be no visible track or road markings of any kind, and it would be easy to become lost. It was near here that the three Frenchmen, previously mentioned, had met their demise.

Our wait for the guide was made quite pleasant by the existence of a hot-water spring that the border police had diverted into a 10-foot-long, cast-iron, cattle-food trough set in the sand. The trough/tub was divided into two compartments allowing two people to bathe simultaneously, and

The hot-water, sulphur spring at Assamaka

since the water flowed continuously, it was always fresh. Clad in our bathing suits, we took turns washing in pairs. To this day, Jean still tells the story about the day she took a bath with a handsome French diplomat.

On the third day of waiting at the border, our female guide appeared. After much haggling the fee was arranged, and we made preparations for departure early the next day. At sunrise, with the roar of seven engines, the convoy struck out to begin its long trek over the 300 miles of barren wasteland.

In anticipation of finally completing the difficult desert crossing, we all left the outpost at great speed. Our enthusiasm soon evaporated, however, when our van began to lurch and then stalled, and we watched our friends in the distance leaving us behind. Repeated attempts to start the engine failed, and the first traces of panic crept into my mind. Would this be the end of our trip?

After a short wait that seemed like an eternity, Robin, Viv and Phil returned to help, while the rest of the convoy carried on without us. All day, in the blistering heat, we tinkered with the engine, but to no avail. Late in the afternoon, though, when the air began to cool, the van started almost magically. We concluded that the fuel pump must have overheated and developed an air lock that impeded the flow of gasoline to the engine. We reasoned that a possible solution might be to wrap the pump with damp cloths to keep it relatively cool. By the time we had made the necessary adjustments, it was far too late in the day to continue travelling, so we made camp where we had stopped, only a few hundred yards from the outpost.

At first light, our small, lonely convoy of three vehicles started out in the direction the others had taken. Anxiously, we searched for the tire tracks that would guide us in the proper direction. Fortunately, there had been little wind, and the tire marks remained visible, so finding our way was easy. All day, we followed the trail of those who had gone on before us, but the day's travel was aggravated by the frequent stalling of the van. To keep the van running, it became necessary to dump water almost continually on the rag-wrapped fuel pump to keep it cool.

A hundred miles or so into Niger we came across a huge oasis, and it was there that we encountered our first band of desert nomads with their herd of camels that easily numbered in the hundreds. From this point onward into northern Nigeria we would, from time to time, come into contact with nomadic people who wandered with their camels, cattle and goats to new pastures and water supplies. The trail through this oasis was difficult to drive on because it was covered with deep, soft sand. To make things worse, it was virtually impossible to drive off the track as it was densely lined with trees and shrubs on both sides. In the middle of this sandy obstacle course, we came upon our Ceylonese doctor friend mired in sand and in despair. He was overjoyed to see us because without help he could not have freed himself, and from that point on the six of us travelled together until we reached the Nigerian border.

In the gruelling heat, we doggedly crossed the barren landscape that was northern Niger. Often, driving was akin to sailing, as we rode up and down the wave-like sandy mounds, sometimes hard-packed and other times treacherously soft. We were fortunate to be in the company of a four-wheel drive vehicle, for on many occasions we were forced to rely on the Land-Rover to drag us over difficult ground.

On our arrival in Agadez, the first town of any size we encountered in Niger, we reported to the customs office where our travel documents were examined for a second time. Upon learning that we did not possess a *Carnet de*

The border post at Assamaka

Passage, the customs officials immediately cleared Jean and I, as well as the Ceylonese doctor. It was almost as though they were thankful they didn't have to deal with any additional paperwork. The same was not true for Robin, Viv and Phil. They were detained for nearly two hours while their *Carnets* were scrutinized. Niger, it seemed, was one country where it was almost a disadvantage to carry a *Carnet de Passage.*

Once customs had finished with us we spent the rest of the day exploring Agadez. We passed part of the day in a simple, one-room bar, constructed, as most of the buildings were, of dried mud. After the bitter-tasting, warm water to which we had grown accustomed on our desert journey, cold beer made a welcome change. The balance of the day was spent in the sprawling marketplace which was a jumble of activity. Rows of tiny shops packed the market square. I use the term "shops" loosely, as these buildings were nothing like western stores. Actually, they were little more than

Nomadic camel herd in a Niger oasis

lean-tos constructed of sticks, reed mats and burlap bags. In front of them, either on tables or mats, were piled the vendors' goods which covered the range of the populace's needs, from clothing and utensils, to meat, vegetables and tobacco. Some of the shops even served as small eating places. That evening, we decided to try one of the "restaurants." The simple, tiny room contained just one rickety, wooden table, surrounded by benches of similar construction, but the food, a very hot and spicy goat-meat stew, was delicious.

In the marketplace, we encountered a young American who claimed he had come to Africa as a volunteer with an aid organization. When he asked Jean and I whether we smoked, we automatically answered "No," only to realize later, during the ensuing conversation, that he meant marijuana not standard cigarettes. Over the years, we have had good laughs at ourselves for how "green" we must have been in those days.

71

As we moved about the towns of old French Africa, native children followed us, constantly begging for gifts; Agadez was no exception. Everywhere, we saw outstretched hands and heard the familiar shrill voices pleading, *"touriste, touriste, donnez-moi un cadeau!"*

The following day, as we continued to travel south again, it became increasingly clear that we were approaching the southern desert margin; the desert landscape was gradually being replaced by scrub and thorn trees. Driving through a low, grassy region, we encountered one of the scourges of Africa, the locust. One minute we were driving contentedly through a peaceful, green landscape, the next, everything was a riot of movement; clouds of the insects were in the air, battering against the van on all sides. We had come upon the swarm so quickly that many of them were inside the van before we could close the windows and the sliding doors, and for a few moments, the interior of the vehicle was pandemonium. Jean and I loathed insects at the best of times, but to be in a confined space with so many of these horrid creatures was almost unbearable. For the next few minutes, Jean was slapping at the bugs that covered her, while at the same time desperately trying to close the passenger door; I was frantically trying to clear the locusts from the windshield, close the driver-side door, not to mention drive the van.

As soon as we returned to sandier conditions, and just as quickly as we had come upon them, we left the locusts behind in that pocket of grassland. The sudden silence and stillness, broken only occasionally by the smack of the odd locust striking the windshield, helped to soothe our jangled nerves. It had been a startling experience, and one that left us nauseated at the sight of the remains of these insects smeared over the interior and exterior of the van.

It was there, on the southern edge of the desert, that a

The camel market in Agadez

short time later we experienced the worst driving conditions of the entire Saharan crossing. Through thorn trees and scrub snaked a narrow, 100-mile trail, down the centre of which was a rock-hard mound, shaped by the wheels of countless lorries. To make matters worse, over many long stretches, the wind had caused sand to drift into the trough-like road. Although I felt the need to drive slowly and cautiously to avoid bottoming on the hardpan, the existence of soft, sandy patches forced us to travel at high speed to guard against becoming stuck. Driving was a nightmare as we hurtled down the road, ploughing through sandy patches, only to have the van come crashing down with bone-jarring force on its underside.

For half a day we bumped and ploughed our way down the track, and even at the speed we were travelling, we were often stuck. Finally, we became hopelessly bound, and I can still remember, with discomfort, the feelings of helplessness and despair we experienced at that time. After a

The marketplace in Agadez

futile attempt to free the van, Jean and I sat silent and deject-
ed until our travelling companions returned. They found us
after an hour of backtracking over two or three miles of that
"hell run." It was at that point that I truly realized for the first
time how ill-prepared we had been for the trip, and how
much of a drawback we were to our friends who always
seemed to be bailing us out of our difficulties. By using a
winch, anchored to a tree, we were finally freed. Having
decided it would be wise to keep the three vehicles within
sight of each other in case of trouble, we pushed on again
in hopes of covering another ten miles or so that day.

Only a few miles further along the trail, we came upon a
car hopelessly stuck in sand and surrounded by a group of
Arab men. To our astonishment, we found that the occupants of the car were two European women, one in her thir-
ties and the other in her fifties. In the ensuing conversation
we learned the women were French residents of Cameroon,
which was where they were headed following a vacation in

France. The Arab band had tried for several hours to free the vehicle. Now the men were becoming somewhat disgruntled at the arrival of the Land-Rover because they thought they would receive no reward for their earlier efforts. One of the French women, noting the Arabs' growing discontent, doled out some money to their leader, and shortly afterward they happily departed.

Using the power of both the Land-Rover and the van, we were able to dislodge the car from the sand in just a few minutes, much to the delight of the two women. To show their appreciation, they offered us a drink, which we all gladly accepted. We had expected a glass of water, and so when they opened their trunk and produced a bottle of whiskey, we were pleasantly surprised. But our treat was not yet complete. To top it off, a flask was opened, revealing cold chunks of ice for our drinks. I cannot begin to describe the pleasure we derived from that cold liquor after the heat and travails of the day.

Following half an hour or so of pleasant chitchat, we agreed to drive on together for a short distance to find a good campsite, as an hour or two of daylight remained. This time, we didn't drive on the road; instead, we drove among the thorn trees and shrubs parallel to the track.

Eventually, we came upon a dry river bed with steep banks and a sandy bottom. Uncertain about how this dry gulch could be forded, and exhausted after the hard day's drive, no one even wanted to try, so we put off our attempt at crossing until the next day. That evening, we invited the two women to join us for supper, and they gladly accepted. In return, later that evening they extended us an invitation to dine with them at the hotel in Zinder, a day's drive further south.

Early the next morning I was awakened by the sound of voices and arose to see what was happening. The two

Roasting meat in the market in Agadez

women were prepared to leave, boldly proclaiming they would show us all how to cross the stream bed. Explaining that the underside of their Peugeot was protected by a metal plate, they climbed into the car (the younger woman behind the wheel), and reversed it several yards to have a run at the bank. Then, with a roar, the car shot forward, catapulted from the bank, smashed heavily against the bottom of the river bed and bounced through it and on to safety. The rest of us stood in silent awe of the driving skill and nerve displayed by the two women.

It was my turn next, and not to be outdone by a woman, I too backed the van some distance, then accelerated forward. Instead of flying majestically from the bank as the women had done, I slammed on the brakes in terror as I approached the brink, and slid sheepishly down the bank into the soft sand of the river bed. All right, I'm not the next Mario Andretti! Fortunately for my ego, I wasn't alone; the others managed to equal my effort, and so our day began with digging and pushing. A short time later, though, we were all liberated from the sand and were on our way once again.

The next stretch of road was truly nightmarish. Fearful of driving on the sandy track, we elected to thread our way among the shrubs and thorn trees. Unfortunately, because of the threat of becoming trapped in sand, we couldn't drive deliberately and cautiously. There was only one course open to us; we flew through the trees with wild abandon. I will never forget that reckless race, dodging trees at high speed and ploughing through sand. It was one of my most harrowing driving experiences in Africa.

Once clear of this treacherous stretch of road, only a short distance remained before Tanout where we made a brief stop at a shop that sold litre bottles of ice-cold Niger Beer. Even Jean, who didn't drink much at the best of times, was able to down a whole bottle. Hot and stress-filled after the arduous drive, I devoured three of them; consequently, the journey from Tanout to Zinder, after quickly consuming such a quantity of beer, was incredible. I led the way out of town, up a sandy slope and travelled at such speed that with no difficulty we slashed through the ubiquitous sand and bounded over the hill. The Land-Rover, however, moving more slowly, faltered on the incline and became embedded in soft sand. So intent was I on making Zinder that I never looked back, and we didn't learn of the Land-Rover's difficulties until our friends' arrival in town later that afternoon.

In Zinder, a shop owner approached us with an offer to purchase our vehicles. At first we were taken aback, but on reflection it made perfect sense. This remote part of Africa had access to few new cars, but situated at the southern margin of the desert, many of the trans-Saharan travellers passed through town. Apparently, after making the southerly trek, many cars arrived in sorry condition, and their owners were happy to find ready buyers.

Sunset on the Sahara

Following the arrival of our friends in the late afternoon, we made our way to the one-and-only hotel where we were told our French friends were staying. Although we remembered the dinner invitation, we approached the hotel unsure whether we were truly expected. Our doubts were soon dispelled. We were directed to a courtyard where a large table was laid for dining under the stars. The animated conversation that evening, combined with a sense of comradeship, the warm, dry evening breezes and undoubtedly the most delicious stuffed aubergines I had ever tasted, yielded a truly memorable experience.

During the meal, our hosts extended us an invitation to visit them for a few weeks at their home in Yaoundé, the capital city of Cameroon. As much as we appreciated the offer, however, it was declined because we felt the side journey would take us too far out of our way, and much valuable time would be lost. Timing was becoming an important issue for us, as we wanted to cross Central Africa before the rainy season. Later that evening, with considerable regret, we parted company with our French companions, never to see them again.

The next day, much-improved roads allowed us to make the Nigerian border and beyond. Passing through Nigerian customs was completely different from our border crossing experiences further north. We observed in Nigeria, as well as other former British colonies in Africa, a certain efficiency and an air of confidence and pride among officials that seemed to be lacking, particularly in old French Africa. Our papers in order, we had no difficulty entering the country. Without a visa, however, the Ceylonese doctor was denied entry and was forced to telephone for assistance to his father in Zaria. Since there was nothing we could do to help our friend, and since all he could do was wait until the necessary documents could be processed, we continued on without him.

The further south we drove, the more vegetation we encountered, and now most of the people we saw were Negroid. Although the Nigerian roads were extremely narrow (equivalent to a lane and a half of roadway in North America), at least they were well maintained, hard surfaces; we felt that at last we had returned to some of the creature comforts of civilization.

Our next stop was the city of Kano, an important regional centre in northern Nigeria, where we recuperated for about two weeks.

Experiences in a
Northern-Nigerian City

K ano is an ancient city that marks the southernmost point of the north-south camel-caravan route that we had followed across the desert. Travellers to the city can still visit the original old town which is surrounded by the characteristic high, mud walls.

On arrival in Kano, we had no idea where to find lodgings, so we proceeded to search by randomly driving up and down streets. After cruising for some time without success, we spotted what appeared to be a school and stopped to ask for directions to a hotel. It was here that we began to appreciate what public education systems were like in some parts of Africa. Walking into the school yard, I passed several classrooms that seemed to have no teacher present, and the students were engaged in what appeared to be idle chatter. My attention was drawn to a class where a teacher was obviously delivering a lecture, and I was determined to ask this person for directions. Not only did he offer instructions on how to find a hotel, but he also insisted on escorting us to the establishment. Eventually, he spent the entire afternoon with us. It seemed strange that a teacher would simply abandon his class to help us; however, we were to learn that what we might consider to be poor attitudes toward teaching and a lack of responsibility were commonplace among teachers and appeared to be accepted practice. We also found it interesting that in many African countries one was permitted to teach school up to the level immediately below one's own education, and without any special teacher training or certification. (Although at the time, we felt that teaching qualifications in general were sadly lacking, we had to acknowledge the efforts that were being made to educate the next generation. One has to start somewhere.)

Our affable teacher led us to the "hotel" which was a simple, two-storey, adobe structure with very Spartan furnishings. In our guest room there were no wall decorations or floor coverings; there was only one wooden chair, and the steel bed springs were covered by an old, soiled mattress.

It was late in the day, nearly dusk, and we were ravenous. Hotel guests had two options for securing a prepared meal. The first was to purchase food from street vendors; the second was to eat in the hotel dining room. During the afternoon we had noticed that many women took up their customary roadside positions where they cooked chickens and yams in large cauldrons of oil, or roasted them over open fires. Although on other occasions we availed ourselves of the food vendors' wares, that evening in Kano we chose the second option.

The hotel dining room, like every other room in the building, was austere. The only furniture consisted of rickety, wooden chairs and tables, and the decor was limited to a monotonous, grey-brown earthen floor and walls. Only one meal was served in the hotel: a fiery meat dish similar to a curry. Jean and I are accustomed to, and very much enjoy, spicy foods, but this was so hot we could barely swallow it. Without the aid of bottles of water to wash the meal down, it would have been impossible to consume. Natives of the area traditionally used cayenne pepper to flavour their food, and we speculated that this explained why so many people had orange-stained teeth and gums.

Sleep was our next priority after eating, and so we returned to our rooms. Only a few minutes in bed were enough to tell Jean and I that we were not alone; the mattress was alive with bugs. In disgust, we leaped out of bed, pulled the foam mats out of the van and spent a fitful night spread out on the hotel's veranda overlooking the street. Eventually, Robin and Viv joined us, but Phil, exhausted, slept through it all, oblivious to the infestation in his bed.

One night's experience at the hotel was all the motivation we needed to look for a better place to stay, and our inquiries led us to the Kano Club. North American and European professionals, many serving as consultants on development projects, congregated at the club to socialize and to avail themselves of the various entertainments. The Kano Club boasted a large swimming pool, outdoor movies and a restaurant, all very neat and clean, and it became our home base for the remainder of the stopover. An employee of the club directed us to the cricket grounds where we were told we could camp indefinitely.

Life during our two-week stay was relaxed; we spent most of our time at the pool, which we relished after our recent desert experience. On a couple of occasions, we attended the club cinema where the films were projected out-of-doors in an amphitheatre surrounded by a seven-foot-high, wooden wall. The moviegoers sat on collapsible, metal chairs, and on the ground, dispersed among the seats, were smoldering mosquito coils to ward off the disease-bearing insects.

Our travelling companions hired a guard to watch over their belongings during our stay. Jean and I did not feel the need for such protection since we were able to lock our possessions in the van. In general, guards were essential for foreigners' homes because, as was the case in many parts of Africa, robbery was commonplace; one might even say pandemic. Widespread poverty was clearly the root of the problem, and foreigners were the most obvious targets as they appeared wealthy to the indigenous population. While the guard was in our friends' employ nothing was taken from them, but near the end of our stay they made a costly mistake. The day before our departure the watchman's services were terminated; that night, our companions were robbed while they slept. someone unzipped the tent, lifted Viv's purse from under her pillow, removed the cash, replaced the purse and zipped up the tent without anyone being the wiser. Phil had been sleeping out in the open under mosquito netting; the thief lifted Phil's trousers from where they lay beside his head. So smoothly and silently were these acts committed that our friends didn't realize they had been victimized until the next morning. It is my conjecture that the locals would not steal while one of their own was hired to protect and be responsible for the safekeeping of property, but once the guard's job had ended, our belongings were once again fair game for anyone bold enough to steal.

While in Kano, we heard many robbery stories from an American who was in the city on a two-year contract as a town planner. One of his tales concerned a robbery at his own home. Like all foreigners' houses, his had steel bars on every window, and in addition, he had hired two guards with dogs to patrol the grounds day and night. One night, somehow avoiding the patrols, thieves managed to enter the locked house and removed many objects from the home, including the man's clothing that was in the bedroom where he and his wife were sleeping at the time. Just like our friends, they didn't realize what had occurred until the next morning. There was, however, one potential consolation for robbery victims. Apparently, many stolen articles were sold to market vendors who in turn put them up for sale. Consequently, if someone wished to recover an item badly enough, he could promptly visit the local native market in an attempt to locate and repurchase the stolen property.

Resident foreigners who left their homes unattended for any length of time expected them to be ransacked. As a result, they were anxious to find volunteers to occupy and safeguard their homes, particularly during extended absences.

Colourful native marketplace near Kano

We heard stories of entire contents of homes being removed while the occupants were away. In one case, the thieves adopted a direct approach to gain entry. They simply backed a truck through a wall and into the house; the dwelling was emptied; and even the fence around the property was lifted.

Jean and I were never robbed in Kano, but one night we were visited by a prowler. We were still in the habit of sleeping with the rear doors of the van fully open with the entrance covered by mosquito netting. That night, after extinguishing the gas lantern, we were lying in bed on the brink of sleep when we heard a rustling noise outside. Jean nudged me and pointed to a shadow cast on an inner wall of the van. A moment later we saw the head of a young boy peering at us from the darkness. We had no way of knowing what his intentions were, whether he was a thief or a *voyeur*, but at any rate, I let out a sharp, "get lost!" and the head quickly withdrew. We were never bothered again.

Many Nigerians were skilled artisans, and close to our camp was a vendor's stall where hand-made leather goods were sold. We found our single dollar bills useful in bargaining, and were able to buy leather handbags for as little as four dollars and sandals for one dollar. Christmas being close at hand, we bought several of these articles and eventually shipped them from Kenya to our relatives in Canada and Scotland.

Near the end of our first week in the city, our Ceylonese friend finally arrived, but he was only able to visit for a day or two before continuing on to Zaria.

After a pleasant week and a half in Kano, restlessness, a desire to be back on the road, set in and we began to make preparations for the continuation of our trip across Central Africa. According to our maps there would be no shortage of gasoline depots on the next leg of our journey, and since our forty-five-gallon drum was no longer necessary, we decided to sell it. With the departure of the large tank, we suddenly found

Leather-handicraft stall in Kano

ourselves with more living space. Also, having rid ourselves of
that store of potentially explosive material, we felt more
relaxed, relieved that our van was no longer a mobile fire-
bomb. The only other preparation we made was to have the
van's engine shampooed to remove the thickly caked layers of
sand. For this procedure, I entrusted the van to a native-run
garage, but that proved to be a mistake. Normally, one would
have covered the ignition system to keep it clean and dry, but
not these fellows. The hoses came out; the engine cover was
removed; and the motor was doused. After this procedure the
engine was clean indeed, in fact it gleamed, but it wouldn't
start. It was an entire day before we were able to dry the
wiring sufficiently to get the van started.

As we looked ahead to the next leg of our journey, through
Central Africa to Kenya, we felt it would have to be easier than
the desert crossing. In many ways, however, it proved to be
the most difficult and demanding part of our overland trek.

The Central-African Trek to Kenya

Ｗe were on the move once again, this time travelling in an easterly direction through northern
Nigeria toward the town of Maiduguri. The roads
were in reasonably good condition as we left Kano, but as
we approached Maiduguri, near the border with Cameroon,
the road deteriorated to a narrow track, and soon we
encountered extremely poor, sandy conditions once again.
(Much of northern Nigeria and Cameroon is savannah on the
southern margin of the Sahara; hence, the sandy soil.)

Not far from Maiduguri, we stopped for our first night out
of Kano. Concerned about our safety, we hired a local man
(armed with a bow and arrows) who offered to guard us

*Herd of longhorn cattle on the road between Kano and
Maiduguri*

Purchasing arrows from our overnight guard

and our belongings. The night passed without incident, and the next morning, we asked our guard to demonstrate his skill with the bow. Taking dead aim at the trunk of a large tree not ten feet away, he pulled back his bow and released an arrow which landed nowhere near its mark, skittering away into the tall grass. So much for our security!

Near Maiduguri we experienced new problems with the van. It had become apparent to us since leaving Kano that the van's power was diminishing, and furthermore, its gasoline consumption had increased markedly. Whereas formerly we had been able to travel about twenty-five miles on a gallon of gasoline, we were now getting half that distance. Since we would soon be in even more remote parts of the continent, this situation was extremely serious, so we decided to stop and attempt repairs.

For two days, Robin, Phil and I repeatedly tried to tune the carburetor and to adjust the engine tappets, but it was no use. The best we could do was to limp along to the next

Distant view of Fort Lamy on the east bank of the River Chad

town where we tried to enlist help. After several hours in a native repair shop, our vehicle showed no signs of improvement. At that point, Jean and I began to wonder, once again, whether we would be able to complete the trip with the van, or whether we would be forced to abandon it. Our only hope was to try to reach Fort Lamy (now known as N'Djamena) the capital city of Chad. In distance, the journey to Fort Lamy was relatively short, but it was still time-consuming due to extremely poor road surfaces. Northern Cameroon had recently experienced heavy rain that had turned the dirt roads into muddy tracks, and heavy transport trucks had gouged deep furrows and potholes in the road, making driving hazardous and painfully slow.

We safely reached the outskirts of Fort Lamy, but to enter the city it was necessary to cross the River Chad which at that point formed the boundary between Cameroon and Chad. There was no bridge available for the crossing; instead, a diesel-powered barge transported vehicles, and

Sunset over the River Chad

small dugout canoes were on hand to carry pedestrians across the river. Phil hired a canoe to transport his motorcycle rather than pay the greater fee for the barge; the rest of us took the larger vessel. There were a few anxious moments as he, with the aid of the canoeist, negotiated the bike into the precariously rocking craft. He did, however, make the crossing without incident.

Fort Lamy was an interesting city. Most of the business people were French, a legacy from Chad's French colonial days. It was a beautiful city with clean streets and bright, white adobe buildings. One great disadvantage to living in the city, though, was the high cost of living. Most people we talked to believed Fort Lamy was one of the most expensive cities in Africa, largely due to its remote location. Virtually all of the city's goods were either carried in by air or by road in transport trucks from Nigeria, and as a result, prices were astronomical. For example, a half-dozen oranges cost about three dollars.

We stayed in Fort Lamy just long enough to have the van repaired: one night and the following day. We didn't actually camp within the city limits; instead, we found a campsite a few miles south, just off the road on the edge of a swamp. That first night in Chad left us with no doubt that we had entered mosquito country, and certainly made us appreciate the anti-malarial pills that we had begun taking daily in Kano. As was our custom, the back doors of the van were open to admit any cool breezes, and mosquito netting covered the entrance. While we passed the evening hours playing cards and dice by lantern light, all manner of flying insects were drawn to the light, and by the time we turned off the lamp, the netting was completely covered and black with bugs.

The following day, a French mechanic discovered the source of our van's problem, a worn carburetor jet. Fortunately, it was easily replaced, and we were able to continue our journey.

WEEK NINETEEN ...

From Fort Lamy, we once again crossed the River Chad, this time travelling south toward the equator. The farther south we progressed, the more lush and dense the vegetation became. The main highway—a dirt road—was narrow, in poor repair and littered with potholes. As we drove through southern Chad, we noticed there were few automobiles on the road, and we seldom saw people except in and around the occasional roadside village. Up to that point on our travels, most of the indigenous people appeared to be engaged in subsistence activities. Now, for the first time, we

Weighing baskets of cotton

observed cash-crop cultivation; here, people grew cotton for export and for income. Many of these villages had adjacent cotton fields in which it was commonplace to see villagers—men and women—tending their crops.

Many Central African countries, including Chad, had customs stations not just at the borders but also inside the country. It was the travellers' responsibility to report to these posts and to have their travel papers examined and stamped. We had always complied with such regulations, so when our map indicated a customs post at Fort Archambault, we left the main road and drove into town.

It was a sultry day, and as usual, to keep cool, Robin, Phil and I had been driving shirtless. Without thinking of the possible ramifications, having done it many times before, the three of us sauntered into the customs hut attired only in short pants. Before we could utter a single word, we were summarily ordered out of the office and told not to return until we were more presentable. Even more surprising was what tran-

Cotton awaiting pickup by truck

spired when we returned to the office of the post command-
er a short while later. He began his interview by asking questions about our backgrounds and our destination. Eventually,
however, he informed us that we had failed to obtain the necessary customs stamps in Fort Lamy; consequently, we would
not be allowed to continue any further into the country. We
knew perfectly well that our documents were in order, and
finally he got around to what we believed was his true interest in us. Repeatedly, he asked how much money we were
carrying, and we became convinced that if we paid him a
bribe he would overlook our so-called mistake and allow us
to continue.

At the end of a long afternoon of seemingly endless questioning, we finally convinced him that we only had sufficient
funds to buy food and gasoline for the journey to Kenya, and
we were allowed to proceed. This was just the beginning of
a series of difficulties we would have with various countries'
officials over the next few weeks.

Cleaning raw cotton on leaf mats

Just south of Fort Archambault, we were forced to make a difficult decision. Our next destination was a town called Bangassou, located in the southern part of Central African Republic on the Congolese border, and when we came to a fork in the road, there were two route options available. Our friends were bent on following a narrow track that was a more direct route, but the condition of the road was less predictable. Jean and I, more concerned about driving conditions than distance, decided to follow a longer, roundabout route to the town, but one that we thought would afford us reasonably good road surfaces. Having made our decisions, we parted company, promising to meet in Bangassou, and we proceeded south into Central African Republic.

Later that day, we picked up a British hitchhiker named Mac who was travelling alone. He claimed to be a mercenary making his way back to South Africa where he said he had once been a policeman. As he travelled with us and as we listened to his patter, we developed the opinion that he was

Tunnel-like, jungle road in Central African Republic

hard, mean and unreliable. At times we worried about his intentions and our safety, but nothing untoward happened during the time he was in our company.

Although the scenery along the route was unchanging, the country's lush vegetation was spectacular. The abundant rainfall produced dense forests and towering trees, and at times it felt as though we were driving through tunnels formed by the thick overhead foliage. Even though the roads were in generally good condition, and we were able to drive rapidly, often we would round a bend near a village and have to slam on the brakes to avoid ploughing through chickens, goats or dogs that were in our path. Not knowing how the villagers would react if we struck their animals, we decided that should that happen we would not stop under any circumstances. Fortunately, we were able to avoid all the creatures on that obstacle course: all, that is, except one. As we rounded a tight curve one day, we glimpsed an enormous snake slithering across the road. So quickly did we

Tributary of the Ubangi River in Central African Republic

come upon it that we bounced over the reptile before I could take evasive action. I don't know if we injured or killed the snake, but we certainly didn't stop to find out.

While driving in Central African Republic, we were continually concerned about being accosted on the road. We had heard that highway robbery was a common occurrence in this country, and that a "rule of the road," suggested to us by other travellers, was not to stop for anyone trying to flag you down. The prevailing opinion was that it was better to be safe than sorry; one would never know, until it was too late, whether the person had comrades in hiding, ready to pounce once the vehicle came to a stop.

An even more extreme suggestion was that we should not stop even if we accidentally struck someone with the van. Instead, it was recommended that we drive on to the next police station to report the incident. The rationale given for this advice was that local tribesmen, in their anger, might attack us. We will never know how sensible these suggestions were, or how much danger actually existed from highway bandits, but we did heed the advice when an incident occurred one evening. Just as it was growing dark, we noticed a man standing in the centre of the road, holding a bicycle upright across the trail in barricade-like fashion. I sounded the horn in warning and continued driving toward him. The man stood his ground until just seconds before we roared through. To this day, I have no idea what the man wanted, but at the time, I wasn't prepared to stop to find out.

Fifty miles or so east of Bangui, the capital of Central African Republic, we parted company with Mac, our hitchhiker, who intended to travel southward by boat via the river systems. We, on the other hand, were turning east for the 250-mile run to Bangassou. At that point, we were close to the equator (about five degrees north latitude), and our chosen route parallelled the north side of the Ubangi River (a tributary of the Congo River) that marked the border between the Congo Republic and Central African Republic.

The weather was sultry and the rain became more frequent. Every day there was a deluge for an hour or so, and the sodden roads were transformed into a slithery, muddy quagmire upon which it was virtually impossible to drive safely. When the inevitable sun finally broke through the clouds, the roads quickly became dry and dusty and were quite passable as long as one didn't mind dodging potholes.

As we drove through the jungle, we observed a variety of fruit trees: grapefruits, lemons, oranges and bananas growing along the side of the road. Seldom did we stop to pick this fruit, though, because usually natives cultivated and laid claim to such trees and their produce. Consequently, we contented ourselves with purchasing fruit from the locals, and for only a few cents, we always had a store of tasty fresh fruit in the van for eating during the day's journey.

On one occasion, we drove through a village that must have received a parcel of used clothing from America. Jean and I chortled when we saw some inhabitants sporting jaunty fedoras but wearing no trousers or shoes; others wore Ohio State and UCLA (University of California) sweatshirts. All of the community members seemed proud of their new attire.

WEEK TWENTY ...

Four days after separating from our companions, we reached Bangassou where we fully expected to find them awaiting our arrival. But a few inquiries in the small town made it clear our friends had not yet arrived. That afternoon, we located a Baptist mission where we were permitted to camp on the grounds for as long as we wished. Chatting later that evening with Patsy, one of the missionaries, we learned of another nearby mission run by five French-Canadian priests. It was such a novelty to hear of other Canadians in the vicinity that we decided to visit the mission the following day.

Late the next morning, we arrived at the Catholic mission and were given a warm welcome by the priests who were delighted to meet us, and invited us to stay for lunch. The conversation at the dinner table must have sounded bizarre for the Fathers, from the Eastern Townships of Quebec, spoke no English, and our command of French was limited. The result was a cacophony of pidgin English and garbled French, but we were able to understand one another for the most part, and our stay, although brief, was enjoyable.

That afternoon we again scoured the town of Bangassou

looking for our friends, but they had not yet made an appearance. Once again, we returned to the Baptist mission where we camped for a second night.

A sign labelled "*Café*" caught our attention as we drove through town the next morning. Just what we needed, we thought, a restaurant, so we decided to stop for breakfast. Walking up the path to the building, we found the front door closed. We knocked, and a few minutes later an old African gentleman answered the door. In our limited French we inquired whether this was indeed a restaurant; where-upon, he motioned us inside and bade us be seated. As we sat at the great table awaiting service, we both commented that this was a very strange restaurant indeed. There was only one table which was situated in the centre of a great hall.

When our waiter returned, we asked for a menu, but he didn't seem to understand, so in different words we asked what there was to eat. He then proceeded to list, from mem-ory, all of the food he had in the kitchen. We chose a break-fast of eggs and toast, which was very tasty, and we thor-oughly enjoyed ourselves eating alone in that enormous room. The meal finished, I called the waiter and requested the bill, but he refused to give us one, explaining that there would be no charge. Instead, all he insisted upon was that we record our names in a ledger to indicate that we had been given a meal. Although we thought this was highly unusual, we complied, after all, it had been a free meal, and a delicious one at that!

Later that day, after spending much of the afternoon exploring the town and lounging around the local hotel where we indulged in a few Tusker Beers, we visited a small general store to purchase some supplies. As it happened, the French-speaking owners, desperate for western company, were extremely friendly, and so eventually we spent the balance of the afternoon attempting to converse with them. During the course of our conversation, they asked if we had been the ones who had eaten breakfast at the home of the local coffee merchant that morning. When we replied that we had eaten in a building we had assumed was a restaurant, the couple roared with laughter. The sign *"Café"* that we had interpreted as "restaurant" meant "coffee" in French. We had eaten in someone's private home that morning! The couple went on to explain that early in the afternoon, the coffee broker had come to the store to ask if they knew anyone named Jones who had eaten at his home while he had been away. The house servant had clearly mistaken us for friends or business associates of the merchant, and although the situation sounded hilarious, at the time we couldn't help feeling greatly embarrassed.

Attempting to pay for our purchases at the store with Canadian money was another interesting experience. The French couple had never seen Canadian currency, and it took some time to explain why there was a likeness of the Queen of England on one side and French-language wording alongside English on both sides of the twenty-dollar bill; they thought it was "funny money." During the course of the afternoon and evening, we became quite friendly, and the couple offered us the store's grounds as a campsite for the balance of our stay.

Three days after we arrived in Bangassou, our travelling companions finally limped into town. We were to learn that the more direct route, that should have taken them about two days to cover, had actually consumed a week of their time, and the tale of their expedition through the jungle on the narrow track was truly a horror story. Heavy rains had swamped large sections of the road and washed out bridges which they were forced to partially reconstruct before they could continue. Needless to say, we were all happy to be reunited.

Zairian villagers coming to our aid across the Ubangi River

The Ubangi River crossing by canoe raft from Central African Republic to Zaire

That same night, the French shopkeepers treated us all to a fine meal in celebration of our reunion. They prepared a savoury meat loaf, and brought us canned peaches and a box of grapefruits to take with us on our journey.

Standing on the bank of the Ubangi River the next morning, we looked across the wide expanse of water to the Congo on the far shore. How on earth, we wondered, could we cross the river? There was no bridge, and the barge, that had at one time served as the transportation link, had sunk years before.

Eventually, we came to an arrangement with the chief of a local village. In return for twenty dollars per vehicle (he insisted on cash rather than trade), his fellow tribesmen would convey us over the river. To accomplish this, several men from a village on the Congo side of the river were summoned, whereupon, they lashed together five dugout canoes, laid a few planks across them to serve as a platform and then instructed me to drive on board. These guys have to be kidding, I thought! The craft seemed terribly flimsy, and they wanted me to put a truck on top of it!

After a brief consultation, we realized this was our only practical option, so we decided to proceed. The chief of the village, who referred to himself as *le Chef de la Barque*, was in charge of directing me onto the raft. Somehow, I found it difficult to put my trust in such a comical-looking person who sported a jaunty cap, wore a tattered suit and pranced barefoot around the newly created craft gesticulating wildly at the Congolese tribesmen who appeared to pay scant attention to him. But, I had no choice, and so onto the planks I drove.

Jean, having almost no faith that the canoes would support the weight of the van as it crossed the river (I wasn't so sure either), decided to remain on dry land where she could supervise the operation in safety. Our fears, however, were

Dense growth of the Zairian forests

unfounded. With great skill, the rowers (four of them, one at the bow and one at the stern of each of the outer canoes) first paddled along the shoreline upstream, and then, at a predetermined location, as they sang and stroked in perfect rhythm, the raft was maneuvered away from the river bank. With seemingly little effort on the part of the paddlers to navigate the raft, the river's current carried the truck to the exact spot on the far side of the river where the road began. Seeing that all was well, Jean had herself paddled across the river in a dugout canoe.

Once the Land-Rover and motorcycle had made the same crossing by raft, it was only a few hundred yards to the Congo Republic's border post named Ndu. But we were unprepared for the next surprise. When we presented our passports to the border official, he told us sternly in French, "You are denied entry. Your visas have the incorrect name for this country!" We couldn't believe what we were hearing. Would we be forced to retrace our steps over the long route

Typical village scene in Zaire

to Bangui to acquire the proper visas? Almost immediately, recognizing the looks of disbelief and pain on our faces, the official broke into a broad smile and told us he was just kidding. Apparently, not long before our arrival (he told us the day before), the name of the country had changed from the Congo Republic to Zaire. Naturally, our visas reflected the former name. Although technically incorrect, our visas were accepted as valid.

Earlier in this account, I explained the significance of the *Carnet de Passage* as a customs document for one's vehicle. In all the countries thus far it had been unnecessary for us to have one, and in fact at times it had been something of a drawback for our friends because of the additional red tape. But this was not the case in Zaire; customs insisted on these papers. Our companions were fortunate. With their *Carnet* they were quickly given clearance to enter the country. As for us, unless we wanted to turn around and travel all the way back the way we had come, we would have to make a

Bantu woman doing her laundry in a stream

cash deposit, the equivalent of 500 dollars (US) in acceptable foreign currency, as our guarantee against selling the
vehicle in Zaire without paying the import duty.

By this time, Jean and I carried about 200 dollars in cash,
most of which we needed for food and gasoline. The rest
was in traveller's cheques which were deemed unacceptable. Fortunately, Phil came to our rescue, offering to loan
us the required sum in British pounds sterling. We gratefully accepted the loan and handed it to the border official who
issued a receipt and assured us that an identical sum, in the
same currency, would be waiting for us at our chosen point
of exit from the country, Kasindi, on Zaire's eastern border
with Uganda.

Although we had crossed the border, a second immigration post was located about fifty miles south in the tiny village of Monga. And what a jarring, nerve-racking ride it was.
The road was narrow, full of huge potholes, and wherever
there was any amount of slope the runoff from torrential

rains had eroded deep gulleys. The slow, tedious drive to Monga took about four hours, and by the time we arrived, we were ready to stop for the day. First, however, we had to clear immigration before searching out a suitable campsite.

Since our vehicles' papers had already been examined at Ndu, it was our personal documents that were of particular interest to this official who was satisfied with everything except for one small detail. Jean's cholera vaccination was valid for only one more week, and we were told we would not be allowed to proceed until this was updated. It seemed easy enough; all we had to do was locate the area's medical clinic and purchase the vaccination. However, when we asked for directions to the nearest clinic, we couldn't believe our ears when we were told "Bangassou." Indeed, the official insisted we return to Central African Republic.

We knew that no amount of debate would persuade him to change his mind, so we resigned ourselves to making the long, arduous journey back to the river and the C.A.R. Our friends, having no desire to remain in Monga, announced they would continue on to the next towns, Bondo and Buta, where we would meet a few days hence. Again, we parted company.

Jean and I immediately set out for the border. Every mile of the round trip, to Bangassou then back to Monga, was mental torture due to the combined strain of the miserable driving conditions and the gnawing aggravation of feeling the diversion was unnecessary. Arriving back at the Ubangi River, we decided to leave the van on the Zairian side and to cross by canoe. Once we found the clinic, the vaccination took five minutes, and then we were on our way once again. By early afternoon the following day we were back in Monga, hurrying to catch up with our comrades.

At this point in the trek, Jean developed a migraine

headache—probably triggered by the cholera vaccine—which was to plague her for almost a week. It became so intense that eventually she lay in the rear of the van while I drove, and with each jolt on the bumpy road, the pain escalated.

Travelling on our own in Zaire, we made it a practice, whenever possible, to camp in mission compounds. In Central Africa there were a great many missionaries of various religions, all of whom made us welcome, permitted us to use their grounds and often offered us meals. One day, as dusk approached, there was no mission in sight. Concerned about camping alone by the side of the road in such a remote area, I stopped at a native settlement and asked the headman if we could camp in the protection of the village. Our request was granted, and feeling secure we crawled into bed, only to be awakened soon afterward by the sounds of scraping and scratching under the truck. Someone was trying to pry loose the spare tire!

Quickly, I leaped into the front seat, started the engine and we lurched forward onto the roadway and off into the night. So much for my brilliant idea of making the village responsible for our safety. That night, we drove on for many miles in search of another campsite, and finally, finding what appeared to be a suitable, isolated spot, we stopped for the balance of the night. The joke was on us though, for at first light, the sound of voices jarred us awake. We had camped only a few yards from another village!

The next day, we arrived at a tiny settlement situated at the edge of a river that we had to cross. Noticing that the barge was at the far river bank, we asked some villagers, standing nearby, whether the craft could be brought over to ferry us across. They replied that shortly, people from the other side would pull the craft over, but it was obvious they were in no particular hurry, so we sat and waited for nearly an hour. (We were to learn that originally, the Belgian barge had been engine-powered, but the motor had broken down many years before. The villagers, unable to repair it, had stretched a wire cable across the river, anchored at either end by a tree, and now the barge was pulled by hand across the river.)

Finally, though, the barge did arrive. Its operators docked close to the river bank, placed two planks from the road to the craft and then beckoned me to drive on board. So far so good.

The short voyage was uneventful, but when we grounded at the far shore, and I was casually asked to disembark, I couldn't believe they were serious. The barge could only get to about 10 feet from shore, and I was expected to drive off into two or three feet of water, then scale the river bank! When I expressed concern, the natives insisted I debark immediately, so we resigned ourselves to what had to be done. Jean, deciding to play it safe, remained on the barge to supervise the operation. Realizing there was no way I could approach this challenge timidly, I revved up the engine, lurched off the platform, crashed into the river and ploughed my way through the turbid water to shore.

Now all that remained was to find a way to transport Jean from the craft to the river bank, as she refused to wade through the waist-deep water. And who could blame her? Taking control of the situation, she commanded the captain, the "*Chef de la Barque*" (as he called himself), to carry her to the river bank. The other men howled with glee as they watched their leader hoist this petite European woman into his arms and carry her through the murky water to shore. Actually, it was clear the man was thrilled Jean had asked him to carry her, and as a reward, she gave him a large, empty soft-drink bottle that we had used to carry water. It may seem to the reader that a bottle was a worthless item

Mother and child: a typical scene in Central Africa

to exchange for such a service. But in fact, in many remote areas, articles such as these were highly prized as they were often hard to come by. In this case, the recipient was most satisfied with the offering, since the stoppered, glass bottle could be sealed and reopened and was impervious to humidity and insects.

As we continued driving, Jean was still plagued by the fierce migraine headache, and so by the time we reached Bondo, some action had to be taken. Fortunately, we were able to locate a clinic where a female, Belgian doctor administered an injection after warning Jean that she might feel somewhat nauseous. Half an hour later, as we awaited another barge that was to carry us across the Uele River, Jean vomited rings around herself. However unpleasant the experience may have been, the net result was that she felt much better almost immediately, and did not suffer such headaches again for the balance of our journey.

Eventually, in Bondo, we were reunited with our friends, and we all carried on to Buta where we planned to replenish our stocks of gasoline. The Buta petrol depot was primitive by western standards. First, we were instructed to roll a great drum of gasoline from a storage area to the pumping site. Next, a hand pump was connected to the drum, and we were told to fill the vehicles' tanks ourselves. (In this region of Zaire, we noticed that the attitude of soldiers and civilians alike had become colder toward us than in the other parts of Africa we had passed through.)

Driving eastward on the jungle roads, we often espied animals, particularly baboons, walking ahead of us. One minute we would see them, the next they would vanish into the forest, obviously frightened by the sound of our engines. With the jungle being so densely overgrown with vegetation, it seemed that, just like humans, many animals used the roads as their pathways.

Because equatorial Africa received great amounts of rain-

Crude, log bridge, common in Zaire

fall, the runoff produced countless streams and rivers, many of which intersected the roads. Zaire, a relatively poor country, appeared not to have the capital needed for road repairs or the construction of concrete and steel bridges in remote areas, and so most small bridges were fashioned out of logs laid down side by side to span the streams. These log bridges created a new driving challenge; it was often difficult to keep all of a vehicle's tires positioned securely on the logs, particularly when the wood was damp. It was easy, therefore, for a car or small truck to slip and have its tires become lodged between logs, and that is exactly what happened to us.

One afternoon, soon after a mid-day thunderstorm, the van slipped on rain-slicked logs, and it came crashing down on its underside, the tires wedged between logs. Fortunately, there was a village nearby, and several men with wooden poles helped to lever us out of our predicament. As a reward, Jean offered a large bag of candies to the men who appeared

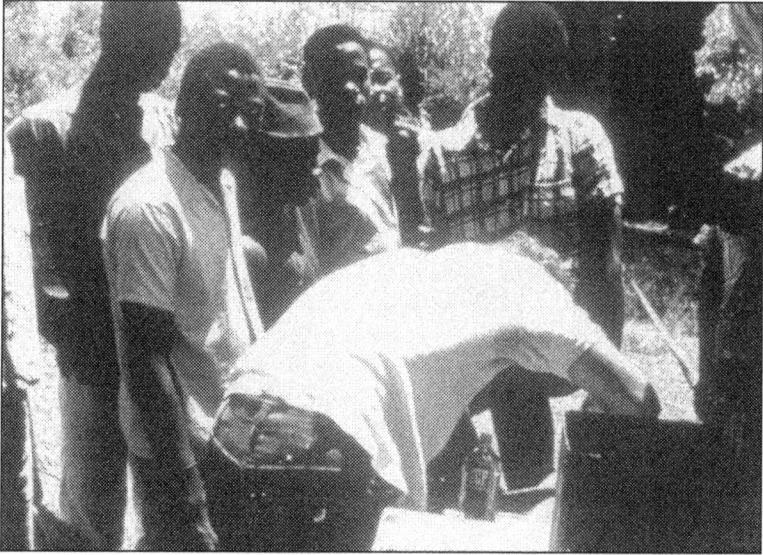

Treatment of natives' wounds was a frequent occurrence

to be quite delighted. Unsure of how to fairly distribute the treats, we decided to hand over the bag to the leader of the group with instructions to distribute the sweets equitably. With that, the man turned, bag in hand, and sauntered off, apparently determined to keep the loot for himself. Jean, furious, leaped from the van, raced after him, tore the bag from his grasp and returned to the group of men who were chortling with glee at seeing the selfish one given his due. Each man was given a handful of candies, and as we drove away, we could hear the taunting cries of the crowd as they teased the greedy man who had received nothing.

Albert Schweitzer truly left his mark on Africa. The legend of the European who could heal the sick seemed to apply to all Caucasians in Central Africa because everywhere we travelled, people came to us for treatment of their ailments. Robin and Viv did carry a fairly comprehensive first-aid kit, and they took the time to treat many of those who were wounded. Unless properly treated, in that hot, humid cli-

Preparation of a maize paste, used a great deal in cooking

mate, any cut, even the most minor, had the potential to become seriously infected. Despite his medicines, Robin's foot became infected after receiving a small cut, and by the time he reached Nairobi, the wound was so serious he was admitted to a hospital where he received penicillin and recuperated for several days.

In northeastern Zaire, apart from the occasional town, most of the population lived in roadside villages. These villages were generally very small, comprised of a few huts constructed primarily of mud walls and thatched roofs. Crops such as bananas, maize and pineapples grew near the dwellings, while other crops, including staples such as yams and cassava, were cultivated in nearby fields. The villagers practised a type of agriculture called shifting cultivation whereby the same piece of land was worked for several years until the soil became depleted and crop yields declined, then new fields were cleared in the jungle.

The village inhabitants didn't eat fruit and vegetables

Banana tree on the roadside

exclusively; they obtained protein from chickens, guinea fowl and goats which they raised. In regions where Zairian villages were located near Pygmy encampments the villagers obtained meat from the Pygmies in exchange for manufactured goods. Since termites provided another valuable source of protein, these small settlements were often located close to termite mounds. In one village, some children were eating live termites, and typical of fun-loving children everywhere, when they realized how much we were repelled by their choice of food, they took great delight in repeating and exaggerating the eating of the insects just for our benefit.

As we passed through these scattered villages, we couldn't help noticing that large numbers of people had great lumps on their necks. In many instances these growths were so large that the people could literally rest their heads on them. Later we learned this condition was goiter, a swelling of the thyroid gland, caused by a lack of iodine in the diet.

Termite mound adjacent to a small, roadside village

The surroundings were lush and appeared to a casual passer-by as idyllic, but the hardships suffered by the people were painfully obvious.

Throughout the day, as we travelled, we ate a variety of fruits purchased from people at the roadside, but in the evening, we usually looked for a village where we could obtain a hot meal. In the late afternoon, women would set up their huge, iron cooking pots to prepare food for villagers and any passersby. Once the delicacies were cooked, we would line up with the village men and pay a few cents for tasty chunks of elephant, wild boar and monkey meat, as well as banana cakes (slices of banana, covered with maize batter, boiled in oil). At the end of a hard day's drive, the local food tasted wonderful.

It was interesting how we came to learn that we had sometimes been eating monkey meat. The locals must have known that many foreigners were repelled by the thought of eating monkey flesh. One day, when I inquired of a vendor

Narrow, tunnel-like jungle trail leading to a Pygmy encampment

what type of meat was in her pot, she spontaneously replied *"singe"* (monkey), but she quickly corrected herself, telling us it was really *"cochon sauvage"* (wild pig). In spite of her entreaties to the contrary, we knew we had been served monkey.

Occasionally, instead of eating prepared food, we would shop for meat in a local market. One day, we all decided to have chicken for supper, so as we passed through a small town, we stopped to buy some. Unfortunately for us, the only fowl available were living, and the thought of having to kill them was not in the least appealing. However, since it was the only way we would dine on chicken that evening, we purchased three birds, each in its own tiny, grass cage.

Later in the day, when we had made camp, Robin, Phil and I went off in search of an appropriate spot to dispatch and clean the birds. I'm not sure whether I was perceived to be the bravest or the most naive of the three, but at any rate, I was elected to slaughter the first chicken. With a single

Temporary Pygmy dwellings in northeastern Zaire

stroke to the neck, I severed its head using a panga (a long bush knife), but instantly, the reflexes of the headless body caused it to leap straight up at me. The sudden shock of being "attacked" by that decapitated creature easily persuaded me that I would never again supply supper in that way.

In northeastern Zaire, we happened upon two Pygmies who were walking along the side of the road. The small stature of the men (4.5–5.0 feet) made Jean feel positively tall. Holding a conversation with these people proved to be challenging because they appeared to use a tonal language of chattering and clicking sounds; nevertheless, we were able to make ourselves understood with sign language. It was such a novelty for us to be in the company of Pygmies that we traded with them to obtain souvenirs of the encounter. We exchanged two empty oil cans and two pairs of my underpants for a crude knife in a woven, grass sheath, a small bush bow and a poison-tipped arrow. The reader may feel that we took unfair advantage in the trade, but it

Members of a Pygmy community

was the Pygmies who felt they had gotten the better of us in the exchange. As I mentioned earlier, containers such as cans and bottles were used as water containers and were highly prized.

Having transacted our business, we offered the Pygmies a ride in the van, and what an amusing sight it was. Both men sat on the engine cover between Jean and me. As we drove, it was apparent they had not often ridden in an automobile because all the while they chattered and gestured with obvious delight and amusement. A few miles further on we stopped to let them out, and as we drove off we chuckled at the thought of two Pygmies scampering about the jungle in Marks and Spencer's underwear.

While in this remote corner of Zaire, we learned about some aspects of Pygmy life from local Bantu and European inhabitants. As was true of most hunter and gatherer peoples, it was the men who hunted and the women who gathered. Hunting was accomplished by several methods. Although the

Pygmies (note swollen bellies from malnutrition)

use of rifles was becoming more common, often the Pygmies used small bush bows and poison arrows (the poison was concocted from the bark and leaves of certain, local trees) to bring down monkeys and other small animals. Nets were also used. A length of netting, perhaps four or five feet high, was stretched through the underbrush. Then, by beating sticks against trees and shrubs and shouting, the women and children would frighten bush animals such as small antelope and wild pigs into the men's waiting nets.

At the time of our journey, Pygmies also hunted larger animals, even those the size of elephants, with spears. Once he had come within spearing range of an elephant and mortally wounded it, the Pygmy may have had to track the huge animal for several days until it died, often far from camp. When a large kill was made, the whole community was summoned to assist with preserving and carrying the meat. There, on the spot, the meat was cooked and smoked to preserve it (a process that took several days), then it was carried in large, heavy packs to the campsite. Meat from a kill the size of an elephant may have provided the people with a source of protein for many weeks, and as well, some of the meat may have been traded to local Bantus.

Generally, it was the women's responsibility to scour the surrounding forest for edible roots and berries. As was the case with all hunters and gatherers, once the game and edible vegetation was depleted, the group moved on to new territory in search of food.

Because of their itinerant life-style, Pygmy homes were merely temporary shelters. When a suitable campsite was chosen, green branches were chopped from nearby trees and were woven into beehive-shaped frames. Next, large leaves were hooked onto the frame by their stems, overlapping each other like shingles to produce a covering that repelled the heavy, tropical rains. Since the buildings were constructed of the surrounding natural materials, there was no reason to dismantle and carry the components to the next site. Consequently, when a camp was deserted, so were the huts, and eventually the campsite became overgrown: reclaimed by the forest.

One evening, we stopped for the night in a small town named Mungbere, about 150 miles west of the Uganda border. Thus far, we had considered ourselves lucky, because even though the roads had been rough, at least they had been relatively dry. In Mungbere, however, we learned that conditions would be quite different on the next stretch of road. We heard awesome stories of torrential rains, slick roads and gigantic potholes. One pothole in particular, we were told, not far from town, could not be negotiated without a four-wheel-drive vehicle. Regardless of this news, we were intent on taking this route because it was the only reasonably direct main road from the town to Uganda. Furthermore, we had no intention of remaining in Mungbere, possibly for weeks, until the road dried. The next day, therefore, we carried on.

Not far from town, the roads became slithery, and soon we came upon a muddy stretch that was gnarled by the wheels of large trucks that had been mired in the swampy muck. This, we thought, must be the monster pothole that everyone had been talking about in Mungbere.

We piled out of our trucks and slogged in bare feet through the mud to survey the situation. On one side of the road there was a four-foot-deep hole filled with water and mud; on the opposite side was a mud-filled trough; and in between lay a narrow, relatively firm, yet slippery passage.

The Land-Rover ventured first, attempting to negotiate that slender bit of firm ground, but its tires were unable to grip the centre of the road. Down it slid into the deep trough. An exhausting two hours ensued as we pushed and shovelled to free the vehicle and move it to firm ground beyond the mud hole.

Now it was my turn. Turning over the engine, I gingerly approached the muddy section, and to everyone's surprise (particularly my own) I drove straight through without becoming stuck. The narrower design of the vehicle had made it possible to stay on the relatively firm centre portion of the road.

Having conquered this muddy stretch, we rejoiced knowing that the worst was over. A mile or so further on, though, we realized that our celebration had been premature. This was the hole they had all been talking about, and it was the

Surveying the situation on the gnarled, muddy stretch of road near Mungbere

stuff of nightmares. The chasm covered the entire width of the roadway. It was about fifteen feet long and seven feet deep, and at the bottom there was at least two feet of mud and water.

The debate about how to tackle this new problem went on for hours. One solution we considered was to slash a trail through the jungle to circumvent the hole, a process that would have taken several days. Another idea we seriously considered was to blaze a trail through the brush to a nearby railway line, drive down the tracks beyond the hole and then rejoin the road. Both of these alternatives were eventually rejected because we felt they would be too time-consuming.

In frustration, Robin started the Land-Rover and drove headlong into the hole in a futile attempt to somehow barge through it. The instant the vehicle struck bottom it became hopelessly stuck in the mud.

Anxiously keeping watch on the clouds overhead, we

The incredible mud hole near Mungbere

strained to free the Land-Rover, praying all the while that it would not rain. We knew that the daily downpour would quickly fill the hole and submerge the truck. Hours later, as we were losing all hope, we heard the sound of approaching engines, and soon two large transport trucks arrived on the scene. The first was driven by a Belgian coffee plantation owner accompanied by a half dozen Bantu employees, one of whom drove the second vehicle.

Instantly appreciating our state of anxiety and exhaustion, the Belgian disappeared into his truck and reappeared with litre bottles of beer, one for each of us. As we savoured the refreshments, the man took charge of our predicament. A wire cable was attached from the front of the lead transport to the rear of the Land-Rover, and almost effortlessly it was hauled backward out of the hole. Next, the native workers waded into the waist-deep muck with buckets and pans to bale out the mud and water. Once most of the ooze had been removed, we all watched as the lead transport plunged down into the hole where it too became mired. Moments later, the second lorry approached the hole. A long, thick, iron pole was secured to its front end, and as the second truck eased toward the first, the pole was guided to a hitching device on the rear of the first vehicle. With a great roar, the second truck pushed the lead one through the hole to freedom, and then one by one, using a heavy steel cable, each remaining vehicle was hauled through that horrendous pothole. Although it was a great relief to be safe on the other side, at the same time we felt sick at the sight of the front of our van. The steel cable had been attached to the front bumper which was now bent into a sharp v shape. Upset as we were though, we could scarcely complain for we were safe, or so we thought.

Dusk was approaching as we set off down the next stretch of road in search of a place to pull over for the night. Though a vast improvement over our most recent experience, the road was still littered with small, watery potholes that we constantly crashed through. As we rounded a corner, immediately before us lay an expansive, water-filled hole, and without hesitation I slammed my foot down hard on the accelerator just as we splashed downward. The hole must have been deep because as we struck bottom, waves of water hit the windshield and flooded in through the engine cover between the two front seats, swamping the inside of the cab. Fortunately, our momentum was such that we literally bounded through and out of the hole without stopping.

We continued on for another mile or so where we encountered yet another obstacle. The road surface was no longer visible. Except for an open swath through the trees, water completely engulfed the roadbed which now looked more like a river. As we ventured onto this stretch of road, we became stuck almost immediately. Unfortunately for Jean (or fortunately for me) only I was able to drive the van with its standard gear shift, so in the growing darkness, Jean, terrified, waded barelegged into the knee-deep water behind the van to push.

It took us several minutes to negotiate that riverine trail, and every moment must have seemed like an eternity to Jean. With every step in the mud and water her imagination ran wild with visions of the creepy, crawly creatures she was sure lurked there.

Just as total darkness enveloped us, we caught up to one of the transport trucks stuck fast in another muddy section; it was time to stop for the night. Without eating or washing our muddy arms and legs, we lay exhausted on the storage boxes in the rear of the van, and within minutes we were sound asleep.

The next morning, the sound of revving engines brought us back to consciousness once again. During the evening, the second transport, the Land-Rover and the motorcycle had lined up behind us, and now all were awaiting their turn at fording the next muddy obstacle. So stiff were we that morning that it felt as though we had aged half a century overnight. The mud, caked on our legs and arms, had dried during the night, making walking and bending difficult until we chipped the muddy shell from our bodies.

As it turned out, getting through the next stretch of road was not especially difficult. Once the first transport negotiated the mud, the rest of us were pulled through. Being second in line, we were soon on firm ground and on our way again. We had arranged to meet our friends at the next mission we came upon, so after a three-hour drive, when we noticed a mission on the outskirts of a village, we turned off the main road.

A sorry sight we must have been as we limped into the mission grounds that day, for when we asked the missionary for permission to camp in his yard, he cheerfully obliged and also insisted that we lunch with him. Knowing that our friends would be arriving soon, we initially declined his offer, not wanting to burden him with feeding five of us. Nevertheless, he renewed his offer, indeed insisted we stay and in addition he provided us with a much-needed shower.

Not only was this man a Good Samaritan, but Father Pascal Palermo—or Father Pay-Pay (pronounced pie-pie) as the natives called him because he loved the fruit of the papaya or pawpaw tree—was a talented linguist. In addition to his native Italian he spoke French, English, seven Sudanese dialects and Kiswahili.

During lunch, the conversation naturally turned to our recent hardships. Phil's motorcycle had been swamped so many times that now the machine could barely operate; repairs were desperately needed before he could continue. Both Phil and I admitted to feeling ill with symptoms of queasiness, together with alternating spells of high fever and chills. Jean was convinced that Phil had contracted hepatitis A, as he had the characteristic yellowish tinge to his eyes. Father Pascal was certain I had come down with malaria.

In Africa, many remedies have been concocted to combat the symptoms of malaria. The Father told us about a local plantation owner who, to reduce the effects of his recurring malaria, would cover his body with diesel fuel at bedtime in hopes of sweating out the illness overnight. Father Pascal's personal remedy was to ingest large doses of an antimalarial tablet at mealtime, and he insisted I begin this treatment immediately. In retrospect, I would not recommend this approach because we were told later that large amounts of the medicine could cause serious side effects, even blindness. It was not until we reached Nairobi that we discovered that, like Phil, I had also contracted hepatitis A.

Exhausted and in need of rest, we were invited to stay at

the mission for as long as we wished, and following our recent ordeal, we were easily persuaded to take time out from travelling. The offer of real beds in the main house was well received by Robin, Viv and Phil. Jean and I, however, preferred to continue sleeping in the comfort of our van.

Father Pascal's mission was extremely poor, so when we learned that the priest was slaughtering his few chickens to feed us, we felt terribly guilty. But try as we might, he would not heed our pleas to spare his chickens; instead, he insisted on catering to our every need.

The day after our arrival, we arose at mid morning to find that Father Pay-Pay had left the mission grounds. Later, on his return, we learned he had walked several miles to a coffee plantation where he knew there was a good mechanic whom he had persuaded to repair Phil's bike. The good priest also informed us that the plantation owner had extended us an invitation to visit him for tea that afternoon.

We were fascinated by the stories recounted by the plantation owner over tea that day. Especially intriguing were his accounts of the widespread violence and the flight of the Europeans (particularly Belgians) that occurred just after the Congo's independence from Belgium in 1960. The land owner was of German origin and was married to a native Congolese woman. During the period of unrest, he had been arrested by soldiers, and because of his colour he was automatically assumed to be Belgian; that meant he was destined for the firing squad. He was lined up with other Belgian men for execution, but was spared at the last moment when someone attested that he was indeed German. After that harrowing experience, his wife secreted him in her parents' village for the balance of that turbulent period. The German went on to tell us that during the time he hid out in the village, whenever soldiers approached, a sentry signalled a warning by drumming on a hollowed-out log. Hearing the warning, the plantation owner was led away into hiding deep in the jungle until an all-clear signal indicated the soldiers had left the area. This man had been one of the few European men in the district to survive, and he had taken it upon himself to manage five other nearby plantations on behalf of the families of his Belgian neighbours who had been killed.

After three days of the priest's hospitality, we felt we could not continue to be such a burden, so we made preparations to continue our journey. Phil, however, had become sicker with each passing day, so we decided to leave him in the care of Father Pay-Pay who assured us he would get Phil the medical attention he needed. Wishing to repay the priest for his hospitality, we donated some money to the building fund for his village church, then we bade farewell to the kind Father and our ailing friend.

Without the three-day rest, I don't know how we would have coped with the next problem we encountered on the road. Only a few hours from the mission, we came upon another terrible stretch. Snaking into the distance, as far as we could see, was a deep, muddy trough that had been gouged by countless truck wheels. For an hour or so, we stood and stared at what lay before us, trying desperately to think of some way to bypass the obstacle. Eventually, we became resigned to the fact that we had no choice but to drive on. The Land-Rover went first, and fortunately, its four-wheel drive allowed the vehicle to claw its way along the trough. Next, we attached a rope to the van's already misshapen front bumper, and the two vehicles laboured up the trail.

All the while, Jean and Vivian walked on ahead, not wanting to look back, sick with worry that the vehicles would either be badly damaged or would be unable to reach firm ground. Although it took a great deal of time, we were able to reach safety, and once again we were fortunate that our vehicles had come through the experience without much new damage. During the course of the journey thus far, there had been at least three occasions when, without the aid of our friends, we probably would have had to abandon our van. To this day, we are grateful for their assistance, for we realize that at times we were a significant burden to them.

The balance of the journey to the Uganda border was uneventful. The roads were rough but dry, and we drove as quickly as possible to reach the paved roads that, according to our maps, began just inside Ugandan territory.

Our exit from Zaire was to be the customs post at Kasindi where we were to recover the 500 dollars in foreign currency that we had deposited on entry to the country.

WEEK TWENTY-THREE...

On arrival at customs, we were told, much to our annoyance, that there was no money for us. At this news, we informed the officials that we intended to remain at the post until they produced our cash. Fortunately for us, the person in command of the post was a junior officer, temporarily in charge while the senior man was on an inspection tour of other border stations. The young man appeared to be worried that we could make trouble for him if our needs weren't met. Consequently, he dispatched a soldier to a nearby Zairian settlement, about fifty miles distant, in an attempt to assemble our money.

While we waited, we were treated royally by the customs staff. Delicious meals of meat and rice were served to us three times daily, and we were provided with beer and entertainment in a grass shack that served as a tavern. The border post was small with only a handful of guards, and since it was isolated, prostitutes were quartered on the grounds as companions for the soldiers. During the afternoons, we lounged in the shack, sipped beer and were well amused watching the women dance the twist and the Watusi.

The good news was that two days later, the soldier returned with money for us. The bad news was that he had not been able to find foreign currency, only Zairian bank notes. Realizing that we would never receive payment in dollars and pounds, we accepted the Zaires and set out immediately to cross the border.

We couldn't believe it when once again a *Carnet de Passage*, or a deposit, was demanded of us at the entry port to Uganda. This time, however, the van looked a mess after its ordeal, and I was able to convince the Ugandan officials that it was worth, at best, only about two hundred dollars. A deposit of fifty dollars was required, which, we were told, could be claimed on exiting Tanzania, the last of the three East African countries on our itinerary. This time, the deposit had to be in "acceptable" foreign cash, or Ugandan currency. At that point, the only money the four of us carried were traveller's cheques and plenty of Zaires, both of which were unacceptable to Ugandan customs. As a result, Robin and I were granted permission to enter the country—Jean and Viv were required to remain at the border—to try to find someone willing to cash our traveller's cheques. After several unsuccessful attempts, we located a shopkeeper of East Indian origin (locally referred to as Asian) who agreed to take our cheques, but at a reduced rate that provided him with a substantial profit. (At that time, in East Africa, there was a raging black market in foreign currency.) With the local money we were able to pay the deposit, and finally we were all allowed to enter Uganda.

School of hippos

Bull elephant foraging for food

Western, long-range view of Mt. Elgon, Kenya (elevation 14,176 ft.)

To our great relief, soon after our entry into the country we reached paved highway, and our maps indicated that hard surfaces existed all the way to Kenya. At that point, Jean and I vowed that never again would we drive on anything but asphalt.

Having been told by the local merchants we met that Zaire's currency was valueless everywhere but in Zaire and Switzerland, we quickly made for Kampala, the Ugandan capital. Our plan was to visit the Zairian Embassy and to explain our circumstances to the ambassador in hopes of having the Zaires converted to some other foreign currency.

Our journey to Kampala, although accomplished hurriedly, took us through some of the most beautiful scenery we had yet seen in Africa. In the extreme west of Uganda, we passed through Queen Elizabeth National Park where, for the first time, we observed great herds of elephants and buffalo on the grassy, tree-dotted savannah and hippopotami in the rivers and ponds. From the hilltops in the rolling countryside

Vendors on the rim of the Rift Valley west of Nairobi

of the southwest, we could see for miles over a vast, open, carpet-like landscape coloured by every shade of green imaginable. Nestled here and there against the hillsides, tiny villages were shrouded by the grey-blue haze of cooking fires.

Occasionally, at road intersections, we came upon nucleated settlements which had developed over the years around a few original shops and open marketplaces, and we ventured into one such village to buy some fruit. In the centre was the marketplace which was a riot of activity. Throngs of people jostled each other to buy bananas, cassava, sweet potatoes and vegetables. After purchasing a few bananas, we continued on toward Kampala. At nightfall we had not yet reached the city, so we opted to spend the night on the grounds of a mission about fifty miles west of the capital.

Bright and early the next morning, we made our way smartly to Kampala where we immediately sought out the Zairian Embassy. After a prolonged wait, the ambassador received us, but only to say he could do nothing to help. He did, however, put us in contact with a black marketeer who was willing to exchange the Zaires at about ten percent of the money's face value. That, of course, was a deal we couldn't afford to make. At that point, our travelling companions, anxious to continue on to Robin's uncle's home on Mount Elgon in neighbouring Kenya, parted from us with promises that we would meet once again in Nairobi.

Jean and I stayed on in Kampala to continue our search for someone who could help us resolve our money problem. Fortunately, after a full day of inquiries, we happened to meet the manager of Barclays Bank in the city. The instant Jean and he began to converse there was an immediate bond, for he too was Scottish. The manager explained that he made regular trips into Zaire, would have opportunities to exchange the funds and agreed to change our 200 Zaires (or pieces of toilet tissue, as Jean called them) for 186 pounds sterling—all of the British money that was in the bank's vault. We were grateful for the bank manager's kind assistance, and we were thankful to have come through the experience with Zairian customs relatively unscathed. We particularly appreciated our good fortune when later we encountered a group of travellers that had experienced a similar problem on leaving Zaire a few weeks earlier. In their case, however, instead of accepting the Zairian bank notes at the border as we had done, they took nothing, hoping to claim their money at Zaire's Embassy in Kampala. They were unsuccessful, and never recovered their cash.

Many times since our African trip, we have been asked for our impressions of Uganda under Idi Amin's regime. Although we were not politically conscious at the time, we did make some observations that can be recounted here. Even in those days, shortly after his takeover, it seemed that some Ugandans privately ridiculed their head of state. While we were detained at the border, we had occasion to speak with army officers, some of whom admitted that many Ugandans felt Amin was an unfit leader who presented a poor image of the country to the rest of the world. One of his actions exemplifies this point of view. While in Kampala, we observed that Amin was constructing a new main street, modelled after the *Champs Élysées*. According to local sources, Amin had visited Paris and had been so impressed by the city's grand avenue that, despite his country's widespread poverty, he had ordered its replica to be constructed in downtown Kampala.

Our business transacted, we departed Kampala, traversed the cotton-growing region of eastern Uganda and crossed the border into Kenya in mid November. After the seemingly endless series of problems we had encountered on our trip thus far, our overriding thought was to reach Nairobi as quickly as possible. There, we would arrange a *Carnet de Passage* and wire back to Canada for additional money. Our route took us through the agriculturally productive southwestern highlands of Kenya. Approximately 100 miles east of the Uganda border, we descended the escarpment into the Rift Valley. There, we passed through towns such as Nakuru with their wide, dusty streets and buildings with high, wooden facades that looked remarkably like many rural towns on the North American plains. Climbing the eastern escarpment, we were treated to a panoramic view of the Rift Valley floor far below, and a short distance further on, we caught our first glimpses of Nairobi.

Our Stopover in Nairobi

Throughout most of the journey across equatorial Africa, we had relied on missions as our nightly refuges. Even in Kampala, we had camped for two nights on mission grounds, and so on our arrival in Nairobi our first thought was to locate a church. We hadn't even considered the possibility that the city would have a camp-ground. We easily located a church, close to the city centre, whose minister permitted us to park at the rear of the property. In retrospect, we probably looked a little foolish, camping in such a location when, as we discovered later, there was a campground on the outskirts of town.

Having established a temporary home base, our next priority was to visit the Canadian High Commission to inquire about the procedure to acquire a *Carnet de Passage*. At the High Commission offices, we spent a good deal of time in conversation with a particularly friendly counsellor who informed us that a *Carnet* would be necessary for entry into Rhodesia (now Zimbabwe) and South Africa, and that we could obtain procedural information from the local automobile club. Since Canada belonged to the British Commonwealth of Nations—as did those countries (except South Africa) through which we intended to travel—visas were unnecessary for the balance of our journey to South Africa. Our last order of business at the High Commission was to leave a message for our travelling companions so they would know where to locate us.

The news at Nairobi's automobile club was discouraging. Before the club would issue us a *Carnet*, we were required to deposit 2,000 dollars, as security, in a local bank. We neither had the money, nor did we wish to leave such a sum in

Tranquil stream landscape in Kenya

a country to which we had no intention of returning. Our only remaining alternative was to ask my parents to arrange a *Carnet*, on our behalf, through a Canadian automobile club. That same day we sent a telegram to my parents in Canada, included all the information needed about the van and requested that they have the documentation processed for us. At the time, we naively expected our *Carnet* would arrive within three or four weeks. We never dreamed we would still be in Nairobi nearly three months later.

Realizing we would be staying in the area for at least three weeks, we returned to the Canadian High Commission to inquire about campgrounds. We chatted for some time with the same amiable counsellor, Robert Hart, who, to our surprise, invited us to park in the backyard of his home. Pleased and comforted to have an acquaintance in the city, we accepted his kind offer.

The Hart's home was lovely. The large, stone house was situated on extensive, treed grounds complete with separate

The plains: a landscape typical of much of Kenya and Tanzania

quarters for the house servant. Although we were offered a room inside the main house, Jean and I, not wishing to impose, continued to camp in the van which we parked in the driveway behind the house.

Even after the first restful week in the city, I continued to feel exhausted and ill, a condition that had persisted since travelling through Zaire. Detecting a yellowish tinge to my eyes, Jean insisted I consult a doctor who, upon diagnosing hepatitis A, immediately admitted me to the Nairobi Hospital where I remained for several days.

Following my hospital stay, the next few weeks of our stopover in the Nairobi area were interesting as there were many new things to see and do, and we were buoyed up by the expectation that soon our one major problem, that of the *Carnet de Passage*, would soon be resolved. During that period we passed our time with trips to the Nairobi Game Park, excursions to the Rift Valley and environs and explorations of downtown Nairobi.

Lioness with her kill

The city was a contrast of old and new. The city centre was crammed with tall, modern office buildings and plush hotels. Tourists and residents alike found entertainment in the coffee shops and lounges of the great hotels, around whose entrances local artists peddled their wooden carvings and paintings. There were innumerable curio shops on every street, most of which were owned by East Indians. Another interesting facet of the city was a street completely devoted to material shops. Cottons from nearby Uganda, lace from France and raw silk from India, all reasonably priced, were some of the bargains that were available.

On the edge of the city, a multitude of mainly small factories produced consumer goods such as textiles, shoes and various handicrafts. We visited many of these enterprises where we observed the production of fine, hand-crafted, wooden and ivory objects, as well as the colourful cloth that was designed and dyed at Maridadi.

Grant's Gazelle

Cow elephants with their calves

Spotted hyenas, scavengers of the savannah

Monkeys grooming each other (removing ticks and fleas)

The unpredictable African (Cape) Buffalo, testing the breeze

Elephants feeding on an upturned Baobab Tree

Impala well camouflaged in their surroundings

Birds of Lake Naivasha (Marabou Storks, Great White Pelicans and Flamingoes)

Wildebeest (Gnu) in the shade of the Acacias

Through the Harts, our circle of friends in Nairobi grew. In particular, we spent much of our time with three families: a young Canadian couple that was in Kenya with the Canadian International Development Agency (CIDA), an East Indian family that had relatives we visited later in Dar es Salaam, Tanzania and an older couple that owned a travel agency in Montreal and had been in Kenya for about ten years. The man, who trained air traffic controllers in Nairobi, was an avid hunter who travelled to southern Kenya each year for zebra and impala. I accompanied him on one of his hunting safaris to the southern plains, and I must say the amount of wildlife we saw was truly amazing. From the hilltops, we looked down on landscapes that were literally blanketed with animals.

In the ensuing weeks we quickly depleted our funds, so it became necessary to send for money from our reserve bank account in Canada. Under Kenyan law, all currency had to be exchanged at official exchanges and rates. There was, however, a flourishing black market, particularly within the East Indian community. These people were desperate to obtain foreign currency because at the time, many of them were being forced out of their businesses and expelled from East Africa. So good were the deals that we could make on the black market that we were willing to risk my parents sending cash to us in the mail, and apart from one envelope containing 50 dollars, all other shipments arrived safely.

Many of Nairobi's East Indians were willing to do almost anything, and had devised elaborate schemes, to obtain foreign cash and to export their money out of the country. For instance, one man offered me a sizeable commission if I would agree to carry a suitcase, containing 50,000 dollars (US), to Switzerland and to deposit it in an account in his name. Obviously, he was that desperate to get his money out of the country that he was willing to take a chance on the honesty of an almost complete stranger. (I had enough sense to reject the offer.) Many East Indians were also willing to risk accepting personal cheques, written on accounts in other countries, in exchange for local currency. According to hearsay, another way of exporting money was through the local casino. Allegedly, some East Indians gambled and lost large sums of money that somehow reappeared safely outside the country.

After a few weeks in Nairobi, all three of our former travelling companions arrived in the city. Robin and Viv had stayed with Robin's uncle on his tea plantation on Mt. Elgon. There, they awaited Phil who had remained with Father Pay-Pay until his motorcycle had been repaired and he had regained his health. We were then able to repay Phil the money we owed him. The journey from Zaire to Kenya had ruined his bike, and as a result, he decided to give it to a cousin who lived in Nairobi; Phil would continue his journey to South Africa by air. Robin and Viv, on the other hand, were about to set off south in the Land-Rover, and planned to traverse the Kalahari Desert en route to South Africa. Still without our *Carnet*, we were unable to accompany our friends, so sadly, we parted company again.

Four days after his departure by plane, Phil was back in Nairobi with an amazing story. He told us that on his arrival in Johannesburg, South Africa, some aspects of apartheid (the system of racial segregation and political and economic discrimination against blacks) immediately began to bother him. On his second day in the city, he said he witnessed a white man verbally abusing a black woman whose apparent "crime" was nothing more than sitting on a "Whites Only" bench at a bus stop. Phil hurried to the woman's defence, sharply reprimanding the man for his reprehensible behaviour. The man, as it turned out, was a civil servant who reported the incident, and Phil was summarily deported from South Africa. Phil's South African experience had been short-lived and his African adventure was drawing to a close. After a brief stopover in Kenya, he returned by plane to England.

As much as we had enjoyed our experiences in Kenya, after two months of waiting for the *Carnet*, Jean and I were becoming increasingly disconsolate, and we felt more and more as though we were becoming a burden to our generous hosts. Christmas came, and the Harts and their friends included us in all of their entertainment plans. During the holiday season we managed to push our worries to the back of our minds and enjoyed ourselves. Despite the pleasant weather and surroundings, though, January proved to be a bleak month for us. In addition to our increasing anxiety about the *Carnet*, we were concerned about our finances and wondered if we would have enough money to reach South Africa.

February came, and finally, the best birthday gift I ever received arrived by mail from Canada. Inside the envelope was the elusive *Carnet de Passage* with an accompanying note from my parents. In it, they detailed the trials and tribulations they had endured in the process of securing the document.

By this time, we were more than ready to continue our journey, so we quickly made our preparations to leave Nairobi.

The Last Leg of the Journey

As we left the city we wondered what driving conditions we would encounter on our southern journey. Our maps indicated (and everyone we had spoken to in Nairobi confirmed) that there were tarmacadam road surfaces on virtually the entire route to South Africa— all that is except for a 200-mile stretch of poor, mountainous track in southern Tanzania known as the "Hell Run." Our first major destination was Dar es Salaam where we were to spend a few days with relatives of the East Indian family that had befriended us in Nairobi. In the rear of the van, we carried a fifty-pound sack of Indian Basmati rice for our hosts, a commodity that was virtually impossible to find in Tanzania.

It was late morning on a warm, sunny day in mid February when we said our goodbyes to the Harts, promising them a letter on our safe arrival in South Africa. In preparation for the trip, I had arranged for the van to be properly serviced, so as we left the city we were confident in our vehicle and looked forward to a quick, problem-free journey.

First, we followed the main highway southeastward in the direction of Mombassa on the Indian Ocean coast, then we turned south onto the highway for Moshi, Arusha and Dar es Salaam; we had estimated the drive to "Dar" would take about two days. As we headed for Tanzania, we marvelled at the scenery. Even the relatively flat terrain southeast of Nairobi, with its acacias and its rusty-red soil, was striking against the backdrop of the cloudless, blue sky.

About fifty miles from Nairobi, our feelings of serenity and well-being were shattered by a loud bang, and the tempera-

Mombassa, Kenya at dawn

ture gauge on the dashboard that indicated the engine was overheating; the fan belt had broken.

All right, I thought, this is an inconvenience, just a minor setback. I must have a spare belt in the tool box. Indeed, I did have a spare, but soon realized it was too small. I couldn't believe it. The dealership where we had purchased the van in Scotland had provided the wrong replacement part. What a way to resume our trip. It seemed as though we were taking up exactly where we had left off—with problems!

Our first thought was to attempt to reach the next settlement on our planned route, rather than retrace our steps to Nairobi. Remembering accounts of nylon stockings serving as temporary fan belts, I found a pair of Jean's and fastened them in place, but it didn't work. I couldn't get the new "belt" tight enough. Next, I tried a piece of thin rope, but when it snapped we resigned ourselves to either walking or hitchhiking all the way back to the city.

Just as we were about to leave the van, a car (one of the

few we had seen that morning) pulled over. The two occupants, an airline pilot and a flight attendant, had been picnicking in the countryside and were returning to Nairobi. The pilot suggested that we remove the pieces of metal wire from some of our clothespins and fashion staples to hold the ends of the broken fan belt together. This we did, and it actually worked for perhaps two or three miles until it broke again. Although disappointed, we had made some progress, so we decided to continue repairing the belt as many times as necessary to make the return trip to Nairobi. The two rescuers volunteered to follow us in case we needed further assistance and perhaps a ride into the city. The fan belt broke and was repaired at least a dozen times on the return journey, but finally, about ten miles from Nairobi, our supply of clothespins became depleted, and the belt, which had begun to disintegrate, was beyond repair. By this time, night was falling, and the couple explained that they had to return immediately to Nairobi to catch a flight. They offered us a lift into the city, but unwilling to abandon the van, we declined, thanking them for all the help they had been. Then they took leave of us, and as we watched their car disappear in the distance, we spotted the lights of a small house not far down the road.

A more friendly and helpful person we couldn't have found. Victor Tofani, a retired fisherman who enjoyed spending much of his time at his seaside cottage near Malindi, north of Mombassa, was eager to be of assistance. With his truck, he towed the van into his yard, and we passed a pleasant evening sharing our experiences, he recounting his life in Kenya, and the two of us describing our African adventures thus far.

The next morning, unable to find a fan belt of the appropriate size in his workshop, Victor drove me into Nairobi where I purchased the required part which we installed later that day.

Sunset on the Indian Ocean coast near Malindi, Kenya

The following morning we were back on the road again. This time we drove south without incident, and that evening we crossed into Tanzania, stopping for the night at a campground in Arusha at the foot of Mt. Kilimanjaro.

Learning about Africa in school had been interesting, but to actually see the places we had read about was another; our early-morning view of snow-capped Kilimanjaro was spectacular. Although the mountain is Africa's tallest, it is frequently climbed. In fact, at the time of our trip there was a regular climbing tour one could take to the summit. For a reasonable fee, provisions, porters and guides were provided, as were overnight lodges located at strategic points on the mountainside. The five-day hike (three days ascending and two descending) took place on the southern slope of the mountain in Tanzania. Jean and I had very much wanted to make the climb. We had seen photographs taken by friends from the summit, and the scene, overlooking the plains through the clouds, was breathtaking. Unfortunately, since I

162

Masai women in traditional red garb

was still recuperating from my bout of hepatitis, climbing Kilimanjaro had been vetoed by the doctor who had attended me in Nairobi.

Much of the landscape we encountered on our trip to Dar es Salaam was similar to many parts of Kenya. One extensively grown crop that we observed was sisal, used in rope making.

In northeastern Tanzania we encountered numerous Masai, a nomadic, pastoral people, who raised cattle and sheep in the general area bounded by the Nairobi-Mombassa highway to the north and the Serengeti Plains to the south. These were striking people with their tall, slender stature and red robes, and many still adhered to their traditional life-style, continuing to migrate from place to place with the seasons. Others had been persuaded to follow a more sedentary existence, growing crops and raising cattle. In the rainy season, they seemed content to inhabit the plains of the Rift Valley, while during the dry season, they sought grazing land on the upper

Nomadic pastoralists with their flocks of goats

margins of the Rift Valley where more water could be found.

The balance of the journey to Dar was uneventful. The second night we merely drove off the road onto a grassy shoulder where we made camp. Although the van was operating smoothly, we were experiencing a loss of power, and the engine, by this time, was burning a tremendous amount of oil. I was reasonably certain the van would get us to South Africa, but I was determined to have a mechanic examine it in Dar before continuing the trip southward.

Dar es Salaam, the capital of Tanzania, was a city of remarkable contrasts. The architecture of many of the buildings reflected the earlier Arab influence which created a certain mystique. Its coastal location and excellent harbour meant that at any given time there were crafts of every description, riding the tide at anchor, from modern container ships to wooden Arab dhows. Coconut palms lined the streets that ran alongside the harbour where vendors sold whole coconuts and chunks of the white, edible flesh to passersby.

Beach near Dar es Salaam

The beauty of certain quarters of the city was in sharp contrast to the filth and decay of others. In some areas, large numbers of buildings were unoccupied and in various stages of deterioration.

On our arrival in Dar, we delivered the gift of rice to the relatives of our Nairobi friends, and were invited to stay for as long as we wished. Although our stay in the city was only four days, our experiences with these East Indian people was quite an education. The family occupied an apartment consisting of six rooms in a five-storey building. From what we observed of the city, their apartment block was in relatively good repair, although there was no elevator. The rooms were simply furnished but spotlessly clean. The two of us were given our own bedroom in which mosquito netting, suspended from the ceiling, was draped over the bed. A slowly revolving ceiling fan kept the room temperature comfortable.

In Nairobi, we had dined on curried food from time to time, but it seemed as though that was all we ate in Dar es

165

Salaam. Our hosts served the spicy meals three times daily, and we wondered how their interest in the food could be maintained. We soon learned, however, about the variety of taste delights possible with curry spices, and our liking for East Indian dishes continues to this day.

With each new country and culture, eating habits and customs changed. With our East Indian friends in Dar, we would be served food *sans* fork, so by necessity, we ate with our hands just like our hosts. Lemon-scented water in finger bowls, as well as napkins, were supplied for cleansing one's hands and face.

Generally, the 50,000 East Indians in Dar took life at an easy pace. Many of them owned shops, and in those days, many young women had begun taking employment as receptionists and secretaries. The work day started soon after first light to take advantage of the cool morning hours. Almost all businesses closed at noon for three or four hours in the hottest part of the day, and most people returned home for the mid-day meal and perhaps a sleep. Later in the day, around three or four o'clock, many shops reopened, some for only a few hours and others until late in the evening. Although many East Indians owned shops, this was not to say that they all personally operated the businesses. Some hired Africans to manage the day-to-day trading, leaving themselves free to pursue a life of relative leisure.

Although we had enjoyed our stay in Dar es Salaam, we were anxious to continue our southward trip. Luckily, one member of the family we stayed with was a mechanic who, on examining the van, guaranteed it would carry us to South Africa, provided we were willing to put up with the heavy oil usage. (By this time, the van required a quart of oil every 100 miles or so.)

Our intended route to Zambia was a 500-mile journey, first southwest from Dar, then through the southern highlands of Tanzania and the dreaded "Hell Run." Once on the highway and driving inland, we were amazed at the large number of Chinese people we saw. Often, we encountered convoys of transport trucks driven by Chinese; frequently, at intersections, there were Chinese road signs indicating Chinese settlements that were rarely within sight of the road; and we often saw rice paddies planted along the side of the highway. All of this seemed out of place in Africa. Later, we learned that the Chinese were in Tanzania for railway and highway construction. Zambia, unwilling to rely on Rhodesia for shipping routes, was building (with the cooperation of Tanzania and China) a railway (known as the TanZam Railway) and a twenty-four-foot-wide highway from the mining regions of central Zambia to Dar es Salaam. The new routes through "friendly" territory would give Zambia access to a seaport.

Large tracts in Tanzania are classified as game reserves, and as we made our way along the road it was a joy to see wild herds of elephants, giraffe, impala and zebra. The southwestern highlands of Tanzania are remote and many of the inhabitants continue to lead a traditional, relatively primitive life-style. Scattered here and there, nestled into the thickly forested hillsides, small settlements could be seen with their typical grass huts and the bluish haze of campfire smoke hanging over the lush, green hills.

It was with great relief that we discovered the so-called "Hell Run" no longer existed. At the time we passed through

Native villages nestled into the hillsides of Tanzania

the area, the highway construction was nearly complete, and all but perhaps twenty miles of road had been paved. So intent were we on clearing Tanzanian customs and expediting our southbound journey, that we completely forgot to inquire about reclaiming the 50-dollar deposit we had made on entry to Uganda and East Africa.

Our entry into Zambia was made at Tunduma. Like many other countries we visited, Zambia mandated that all travellers in motor vehicles purchase automobile insurance at the border. Admittedly, the cost of the insurance was reasonable, but at that time we were short of funds; we only carried about 75 dollars, just enough to buy food and gasoline, with a small reserve for emergencies. In an effort to avoid paying this fee, we attempted to bluff our way into the country. When asked for the insurance fee, we produced our one-month's insurance slip from Britain, explaining to the customs official that the coverage was still valid, and that our insurance company would cover us anywhere in the world.

Burchell Zebra and Masai Giraffe

Of course this was an outright falsehood; the document clearly stated it only covered us in Britain for thirty days. Our story must have been convincing, though, because we were not pressed further, and were permitted entry to Zambia.

Apart from our stay with friends in Dar es Salaam, on our southern trek we elected to camp each night at the side of the road. This was partly due to the fact that there were fewer foreign missions, and also because the existence of paved highway gave us a heightened sense of security.

Our journey down the length of central Zambia was exceedingly uninteresting, as there was little to see along our chosen route. In our haste, we travelled the main road where there were few settlements and few people, and on both sides of the highway there were seemingly endless stands of tall forests. We were to learn that part of the explanation for the relatively low population density of northern Zambia was the existence of mining operations for copper, lead and zinc in the central region north of Lusaka. Apparently, Zambians, in large numbers, were lured to the mining towns with expectations of finding employment and perhaps higher wages than were found elsewhere in the country.

Following our swift and uneventful drive through Zambia, we crossed the border into Rhodesia at Chirundu near the Kariba Dam where both Rhodesia and Zambia had constructed hydro-electric power stations. We followed this route because it was the most direct to Salisbury (now known as Harare), Rhodesia's capital. Had we not felt the necessity to travel hastily, we might have taken the longer, more scenic route via Livingstone and Victoria Falls on the Zambezi River.

Although we experienced no difficulty entering Rhodesia, the customs officials warned us that at the South African frontier we would have to demonstrate our ability to financially support ourselves while in the country. That meant we would be required to have a minimum of 500 dollars in our possession to gain entry to South Africa. Having so little cash on hand, it was clear we would have to stop in Salisbury and wire back to Canada for additional funds.

The 150-mile drive from the Zambian border to Salisbury took us through predominantly agricultural land where the growing of maize and dairy farming appeared to be the chief agricultural pursuits.

Almost immediately after entering the country, we were stopped by a barricade across the road. The person in charge of the roadblock ordered us into a nearby shed where another person opened the van's doors and began spraying the inside of the vehicle. At the time I thought, we may look a bit grubby, but this is carrying things a little too far! The spraying completed, we were directed to leave the shed, and a short distance down the highway, a road sign provided an explanation of what we had experienced. What we had driven through was a control point to eradicate any tsetse flies that may have been carried by the vehicle. This insect carries

Rainbow over Victoria Falls

parasites that, if transmitted to animals or humans, can cause sleeping sickness, potentially leading to death if left untreated.

Victoria Falls viewed from the south

WEEK THIRTY-FOUR...

Salisbury was a beautiful city with clean, well-kept buildings and immaculate streets. At the time, we remarked that this was the most attractive city we had seen in Africa. Because we arrived in the late afternoon, we made for the city's campground which was located close to the downtown. The following morning, we were off in search of a post office where we could send a telegram to our Canadian bank requesting money. The transfer of money took more than a week, but the delay afforded us time to explore the city and its environs.

The downtown sector was comprised of government offices, office blocks and the usual *mélange* of department stores and smaller shops, and we spent a great deal of our time rummaging through the many bookstores, copperware shops and restaurants. The local Bantu population was, for the most part, better dressed and better educated than those in most other African countries that we had visited. Stately European-style residences and native housing areas were located in the suburbs; generally, industry was found on the periphery of the city.

The industry of Salisbury was mainly of the light manufacturing variety such as textiles and clothing. Most of the heavy industry, such as iron and steel, coincided with the major mining belt, a 300-mile band between Salisbury and the town of Bulawayo to the southwest. To a large extent, the absence of heavy industry in Salisbury contributed to its relative cleanliness. Many of the conveniences we had been accustomed to in Canada, we found in Salisbury, including drive-in cinemas which we visited on a couple of occasions.

When we were not touring the town, our time was spent at the campsite. Temperatures in February were still quite warm, so we found the camp swimming pool a welcome diversion. Any campground is a sure place to meet people, and during our stopover we made many new acquaintances. One family we met was from British Columbia, Canada. The young couple and their two small children (he was a fisherman) had bought a Volkswagen van in Germany, driven through southern Europe to India, boarded a ship in Bombay for a voyage to Mombassa and travelled roughly the same route we had followed through East Africa and Zambia to Rhodesia. When we encountered them, they were en route to South Africa where they planned to board another ship for a return voyage to Vancouver.

Another day we met two young British men who had obtained work visas and immigration papers for South Africa. Much to our surprise, they had traversed the continent by the same route we had taken, so we passed many hours sharing stories with them.

Finally, just before leaving Salisbury, we met a retired couple who intended to drive northward to Europe, following the same jungle and desert route we had travelled. Although we admired their courage, we felt compelled to advise them of the physical and psychological demands of the journey. In addition, we warned them about the difficulties they might encounter travelling through newly independent African countries with Rhodesian passports. Our best advice was that they should sail to India, then drive on paved highway all the way to Europe. We have no idea what decision they made or what became of them.

A t last our money arrived, and we were able to continue the trip. The weather was fine, the roads were excellent and it was only a short run, just over 350 miles, to the South African frontier at Komatipoort. Without immigration papers, we lied about our intentions when we reached South African customs. We declared that we had no intention of remaining long in South Africa, but rather that we were tourists who planned to continue our trip up the continent's west coast. Of course we knew all along that within the two-week period allowed us on a visitors' permits, we would apply for permanent residency status. The customs officials, satisfied that we had sufficient funds in our possession to be self-supporting, and having searched the van thoroughly for illegal substances and banned publications like *Playboy* magazine, allowed us to proceed. At last, we made our triumphant entry into South Africa. That evening, we camped just inside the border, and the next day we made the easy 250-mile drive to Johannesburg.

Our gruelling yet fascinating 10,000-mile trek down the length of Africa was at an end. During most of the trip there had been too many nerve-shattering situations for us to say we had enjoyed the experience. But after completing the journey, and in retrospect, it was an experience that we will fondly remember.

They say that once you have visited Africa there is some force that beckons you back. Over the intervening years we have felt that urge, and I am confident that one day we will return.

The triumphant entry into South Africa

Yes, Jean and I did stay in South Africa, where we lived, worked and travelled during an eventful year, but that's another story.

Postscript

It's a small world, full of coincidences. Six years later, having had no contact with him since Kenya, Jean and I had a chance encounter with Robin on a busy street in Riyadh, Saudi Arabia where we were working for an American consulting firm. After crossing the Kalahari Desert and spending a period of time in South Africa, Robin had worked for two or three years in Libya, during which time he traversed the Sahara twice more. He and his American wife were teaching English at Riyadh University. Following his return to England, Phil trained to teach English as a Second Language (ESL), and the last we heard, he was teaching in Japan.